PL

ANGELS OF LIGHT, ANGELS OF GOODNESS, ANGELS OF LOVE

"I was astonished when my angel spoke up loud and clear inside my head. *She is the one for you. She is the one selected as your help-mate on your life path.* And my angel was right. Ours is a marriage truly made in heaven."

— Dave Ragan

"After more than ten years together, we are still very much in love. My angel guide says that Charles and I are like two white horses prancing together."

— Lori Jean Flory

"With each passing day, it becomes clearer to me that Sherry and I have truly become living crystals of Light and Love. Oh, there have been difficult times and dark nights of the soul, but we know that the Angels of Love have blessed us."

— Brad Steiger

INFORMATIVE—
COMPELLING—
SCINTILLATING—
NON-FICTION FROM PINNACLE TELLS THE TRUTH!

BORN TOO SOON (751, $4.50)
by Elizabeth Mehren
This is the poignant story of Elizabeth's daughter Emily's premature birth. As the parents of one of the 275,000 babies born prematurely each year in this country, she and her husband were plunged into the world of the Neonatal Intensive Care unit. With stunning candor, Elizabeth Mehren relates her gripping story of unshakable faith and hope—and of courage that comes in tiny little packages.

THE PROSTATE PROBLEM (745, $4.50)
by Chet Cunningham
An essential, easy-to-use guide to the treatment and prevention of the illness that's in the headlines. This book explains in clear, practical terms all the facts. Complete with a glossary of medical terms, and a comprehensive list of health organizations and support groups, this illustrated handbook will help men combat prostate disorder and lead longer, healthier lives.

THE ACADEMY AWARDS HANDBOOK (887, $4.50)
An interesting and easy-to-use guide for movie fans everywhere, the book features a year-to-year listing of all the Oscar nominations in every category, all the winners, an expert analysis of who wins and why, a complete index to get information quickly, and even a 99% foolproof method to pick this year's winners!

WHAT WAS HOT (894, $4.50)
by Julian Biddle
Journey through 40 years of the trends and fads, famous and infamous figures, and momentous milestones in American history. From hoola hoops to rap music, greasers to yuppies, Elvis to Madonna—it's all here, trivia for all ages. An entertaining and evocative overview of the milestones in America from the 1950's to the 1990's!

Available wherever paperbacks are sold, or order direct from the Publisher. Send cover price plus 50¢ per copy for mailing and handling to Penguin USA, P.O. Box 999, c/o Dept. 17109, Bergenfield, NJ 07621. Residents of New York and Tennessee must include sales tax. DO NOT SEND CASH.

ANGELS OF LOVE

BRAD STEIGER

PINNACLE BOOKS
WINDSOR PUBLISHING CORP.

PINNACLE BOOKS are published by

Windsor Publishing Corp.
850 Third Avenue
New York, NY 10022

First Printing: January, 1995

Printed in the United States of America

TABLE OF CONTENTS

Acknowledgments

I would like to acknowledge the assistance of many individuals who extended their full cooperation in the preparation of the text. In particular, I'd like to thank the many disciples of the Angels of Love who generously shared their personal stories with me for this book.

My appreciation must also be extended to Marvel Ruth Clark, Mary-Caroline Meadows, Stan Kalson, Timothy Green Beckley, and Dr. Allen Nelson Haimes. Deepest regards and love are expressed to the memory of Fay Marvin Clark and Victor Darr.

In addition, I must thank Paul Dinas, Executive Editor of Pinnacle Books, for his unbridled enthusiasm for the project; my agent, Agnes Birnbaum, for her unfailing support of my work; and, of course my inspiration, soulmate and wife Sherry, whose wise counsel is one of my strongest bulwarks against the stresses of life on the earth plane. Neither must I forget to express a very warm prayer of thankfulness to the Angels of Love themselves for their inspiration and guidance during the writing of this book.

Introduction

It seems that it is important to God's plan for the evolution of planet Earth that certain humans come together as man and wife, lovers, soulmates, or parents of children. On occasion, in order to accomplish this particular kind of mission, some intervention from beyond our human world is needed. Some call these intercessors the Angels of Love, beings who assume various disguises and identities and help couples fulfill their spiritual and romantic destinies.

Numerous texts from the vast annals of antiquity inform us that this mysterious cosmic interest in the pairing of particular humans has been going on for centuries. The book of Tobit (*circa* 622 B.C.), one of the Apocryphal texts of the Bible, relates an interesting story of the angel Raphael who was assigned the task of uniting two young people in marriage. The Lord made it very clear to the angel that it was up to him to see to it that Tobias, the son of the faithful and devout merchant Tobit, became the husband of the lovely maiden Sarah.

Raphael's mission was made even more complex by the very unpleasant fact that the awful demon Asmodeus was also fond of Sarah and possessive of her. The vicious angel of darkness had already killed seven young men who had sought Sarah's hand in marriage.

Although the demon had not yet touched or defiled the young woman's body or her soul, he had staked Sarah out as his own and was saving her for a special cosmic occasion when he might fully satisfy his satanic lust.

The text of the book of Tobit is fascinating in many regards, but surely the clear message that humans may attract the attention of both the angels of light and of darkness is of vital importance to those who may from time to time indiscriminately seek love in all the wrong places. Although the present book is devoted to extolling the efforts of the angels of love and light, we shall be certain to include a few cautionary chapters detailing negative encounters and providing you, the reader, with the proper ways to test the entities that may appear to assist you in the selection of a worthy lover, mate, or marriage partner.

In the case of Tobias, Raphael assumed the name of Azarias and masqueraded in the role of kinsman to Tobit. Since, to add to his torments, Tobit had been accidentally blinded, Raphael told the pious merchant that he would be pleased to serve as the guide who would accompany Tobias to the arms of the beautiful Sarah.

The angel on assignment took advantage of the travel time on the journey with Tobias to instruct the young man in the mastery of certain rituals and prayers that were especially designed to keep away evil spirits, to cure various diseases, and even to remove the cataracts from his father's eyes upon his return home.

Appearing to all those humans he chanced to meet as but an ordinary man possessed of extraordinary resourcefulness, Raphael continued in his disguise as kinsman to Tobias and effectively guided the traditional Jewish courtship right up to the much anticipated wedding night.

Although he had provided Tobias with a special incense designed to ward off evil spirits, Raphael took no chances with any devilish interference on the part of the lustful and possessive Asmodeus. The angel of love and light quickly overcame his demonic adversary, bound him securely, and carried him off to a desert in upper Egypt.

Alone with his bride, Tobias asked the Lord's blessing upon their marriage and proclaimed his assurances to God that he did not take Sarah as his wife for "any lustful reason, but solely that our children may bless your name for ever and ever."

Sarah beseeched God that she and her husband might "both grow old together," for they had become one as "the children of holy ancestors."

Numerous times in the last couple of decades the Vatican has made official pronouncements defending the concept that each human being has a guardian angel to assist him or her in leading a good life.

Although the strictly orthodox religionists are somehow able to dissociate their guardian angels from the mystical concept of spirit guides, masters, and teachers, I believe that it is clearly a matter of semantics and religious-cultural prejudices which determines the title that one assigns to those multidimensional beings who, for some reason, concern themselves with the activities of us mortals.

In addition to the above-mentioned spirit guides, there are the *bodhisattvas* of Buddhism, those beings who have earned Nirvana but who stay behind to help suffering humanity; the *garudas* and *asparas,* of the

Hindu; the *valkyries* of the Norse; the *shakti* and *peris* of the Persians; and the *daemones* of the Ancient Greeks—to name only a few.

And in modern times, we must add such titles as Light Beings, Star Beings, and Space Brothers, the wise and benevolent teachers who allegedly come from Outer Space, to the long list of entities who seem to take an active role in shepherding us mortals to higher consciousness.

In this book, we are concerned only with those Angels of Love who are seemingly most intent upon getting certain mortals together as lovers, spouses, and future parents. And while you may see from time to time in the text, references made to Space Brothers, Light Beings, spirit guides, and even spirits of deceased loved ones who appear to be acting the roles of guardian angels, I am now reiterating my position that they are essentially the same kind of entity. *How* they appear may be solely in the eye of the beholder.

I remember discussing the subject of angelic visitations and manifestations with Harold Schroeppel, a friend who used to have a metaphysical center in the Chicago area.

Harold perceived such intelligences as angels to be "intending forces," energies or intelligences that had a definite intention of bringing about some event, of causing something to happen on the Earth plane.

"Now *how* my students might perceive this intelligence would depend upon their previous preconceptions. Most of our students would probably see the entities as lights. However, if certain students were spiritualists, let us say, the chances are they would probably perceive the agency that brought them messages as looking like an American Indian spirit guide, complete with feathered headdress—because this is what they would expect to see.

"I think these things (i.e., angelic messengers) are forces or force patterns, and that individuals 'read out' what images are acceptable to them. If a person is Jewish, the mechanism may appear as Father Abraham. If he expects an angel, that's what he gets."

Since 1968, I have been distributing a questionnaire to the readers of my books and to those who have attended my lectures and seminars. At this time, well over 20,000 men and women have returned the "Steiger Questionnaire of Mystical, Paranormal, and UFO Experiences," and quite a remarkable picture appears of the number of individuals who feel that they have encountered angels, guides, Light Beings, and other supernatural companions.

38% have reported the visitation of an angel.

37% reveal the manifestation of a Light Being.

35% feel that they were blessed by the appearance of a Holy Figure.

50% are convinced that they have a personal spirit guide or guardian angel.

40% admit to having had an "invisible playmate" as a child.

20% state that they spotted an elf or fairy as a child.

20% have perceived devas or nature spirits.

14% claim to have quite regularly witnessed the activities of the fairy folk, the "gentry."

34% are certain that they have encountered alien entities of an extraterrestrial or multidimensional nature.

22% feel that their parents were brought together by an angel, spirit guide, or extraterrestrial/multidimensional entity.

30% are certain that they themselves were guided to a specific lover, mate, or spouse by an angel, spirit guide or extraterrestrial/multidimensional entity.

* * *

Although I shall use the term "angel" consistently throughout this book as the most convenient and universal designation of the intelligence at work in bringing certain men and women together as couples enveloped in the love vibration, I wish to point out that our Angels of Love may wear many different costumes in order to more effectively play cupid and accomplish their earthly mission.

Having successfully brought about a proper marriage and banished the demon Asmodeus from Sarah's life, Raphael continued to maintain his human disguise until he had brought the young couple safely into the arms of the eagerly awaiting Tobit. Then, after presiding over the healing of the blinded merchant's eyes, the angel revealed himself when the grateful Tobit sought to reward him for all his kindnesses.

"I am Raphael, one of the seven angels who stand before the Lord," he told them.

When father and son immediately prostrated themselves in awe before him, the angel told them that they need have no fear. The faithful Tobit had found favor with God, and he, Raphael, had been sent to heal him and to remove the demon from the girl who was to be his daughter-in-law.

"If I seemed to eat and drink with you," Raphael said, "it was only your imagination.

It is time now that I must return to the one who sent me."

And then, after having spent many weeks living undetected among his human "kinsmen" as one of them, Raphael disappeared before their astonished eyes.

How many thousands of couples have the Angels of Love brought together over the past 50,000 years or so?

And were these couples brought together because of their "holy ancestry," as Sarah suggested? Or as so many philosophers have wondered, do the Angels of Love assist us in finding our true soulmates, our actual "other half?" As the great thinker Swedenborg declared, "Two consorts in Heaven are not two, but one angel."

Were you aware of angelic interaction in the creation of your own love relationship?

Could your marriage or relationship have been angelically arranged like that of the union of Tobias and Sarah?

Maybe the inspired minstrel who first observed that marriages are made in Heaven was being more prophetic than poetic.

As you read the stories in this book from men and women who share their own encounters with Angels of Love, you just might be reminded of a mysterious person who briefly touched the lives of you and your loved one. You, too, may remember that you also entertained an Angel of Love unaware.

Part One

Angels of Love: Heavenly Matchmakers

One

Sherry, My Gift from Heaven

In October of 1986, I could no longer endure a marriage that had steadily progressed from psychic torment to psychological torture. The beautiful home in Scottsdale, Arizona, complete with swimming pool and a lush Oriental garden on which I had invested so much time and effort, could no longer compensate for the spiritual anguish which the soured relationship had inflicted upon me. I moved out of the house and into an apartment in Phoenix, determined to reclaim my dignity and self-respect.

A few weeks later, I was beginning to yield

to the entreaties of my friend, Stan Kalson,
to "get back into the flow of life."

Stan, the Director of the International Ho-
listic Center in Phoenix, has always been at
the cutting edge of research in nutrition and
alternate health care; and on this occasion he
was sponsoring a demonstration conducted
by Dr. Caruso, a remarkable practitioner of
polarity therapy who, though well into his
eighties, was still actively engaged in the healing arts. I hadn't given Stan a firm commitment about whether or not I would attend
the demonstration, but since it was being
held at Herb and Ann Puryear's metaphysical
center only a short distance from my apartment, I decided at the last minute to go.

I took a seat in the front row so that Stan
would be certain to see that his well-inten-
tioned urgings to pry me away from non-stop
work in my apartment had been successful,
but I truly did not feel at all like being social
or mixing with the crowd. I knew that I
would be meeting Dr. Caruso after the program for a quiet evening of conversation at
Stan's home, but I really hoped that my
friend had no hidden agendas up his sleeve.
My basic attitude toward any member of the
opposite sex at this particular time of emotional chaos was one of extreme caution and
more than a little distrust.

Just before the evening's proceedings were

to begin, an attractive blond lady approached me and asked if I were Brad Steiger. When I admitted that I was, she proceeded to introduce herself: "I am Mary-Caroline Meadows. Is the seat next to you taken?"

The pretty woman exuded a great deal of charm, so I was pleased to tell her that she was welcome to sit in the empty chair beside me. After all, there might as well be a pleasant person sitting next to me as someone as dour as I was feeling.

Then Mary-Caroline turned to me and uttered the words that transformed my attitude from depressed and negative to optimistic and positive. "I must tell you that I bring you greetings from our very dear mutual friend, Sherry Hansen."

My charming new acquaintance suddenly had my complete attention. I had really only met Sherry Hansen once before, and I had thought her the most beautiful, fascinating, and captivating woman that I had ever seen. What was more, even though our brief meeting had taken place over four years before, I had not been able to get her out of my mind. And one of the basic reasons for that fixation was the peculiar fact that her image had been placed in my mind after a paranormal happening when I was a boy of five—forty-five years ago.

"Is Sherry Hansen here in Phoenix?" I asked Mary-Caroline incredulously.

In 1982, Sherry had stopped by my office in the company of her producer. At that time she had been on her way to Europe on business. She had read one of my books and had wanted to meet me. She was living at that time in Los Angeles. I assumed that she still was.

"Why, yes, Sherry is here in Phoenix," Mary-Caroline said. "In fact, we take a class together. And last night in class, when I said that I would be seeing you tonight at Dr. Caruso's lecture, she said to be certain to say hello to you and to give you her love."

I was suddenly so excited to learn that Sherry Hansen was in Phoenix that my normally rational journalist's mind did not wonder how Mary-Caroline Meadows, who was meeting me for the first time, could possibly have known that she would see me at the lecture that evening. Especially since I myself hadn't known until minutes before the presentation began, that I would be there.

But my capacity for analysis had been completely suspended by my mental vision of the enchanting Sherry Hansen— and the thought that she cared enough about me to send her greetings with a friend.

Stan Kalson introduced his mentor, Dr.

Caruso, and the energetic octogenarian began his demonstration.

I'm afraid that I observed with only a portion of my conscious attention. My memory was churning up some uncomfortable images of my awkward first meeting with Sherry.

I had recognized her as the fairy princess of my childhood visions the second that she stepped into my office.

But as fate would have it, when I met her in 1982, I was so miserable emotionally that I held myself aloof from her.

My marriage had disintegrated into bitter estrangement. My acute embarrassment at the failure of the relationship kept me in the relationship far too long, and I desperately attempted to keep up appearances.

At the time that I met Sherry, I was the president of Harmonious Publishing Company, producing other people's books and cassette tapes— while striving to maintain my own career as an author, lecturer, and psychical researcher.

Most evenings, after having worked on my duties for the company from ten to five, I would start work on my own writing projects after a brief dinner break. Sometime in the hours before dawn, I would often doze off at my typewriter and spend what remained of the night asleep on the floor beside my desk. Daily, I was forced to deal with the stresses arising from the financial problems of the company, the individual temperaments of the staff, the eccentricity of one of our principal backers, and the fickle demands of the marketplace.

When Sherry walked into my office that day, I treated her quite brusquely. But while I maintained a cool, unruffled exterior demeanor, inwardly I was screaming in frustration: "Dear God, why did you bring her into my life *now*? I am already nearly out of my mind trying to balance the cascading pieces of a crumbling reality. Why torment me further by parading the woman of my dreams in front of my eyes when I can't touch her or even tell her how much she means to me!"

I could scarcely look at Sherry, for fear I would suddenly leap to my feet, scoop her up in my arms, toss her over my shoulder and run off to the mountains with my prize— while advising the rest of my world where it could go.

It would have been unfair to Sherry to encourage any kind of relationship— even a platonic friendship— while I was so depressed. At this point in my life, I had begun believe that I was living under a curse that had somehow been set in motion by my marriage— and maybe I really was.

What I did not fully realize at the time was that if the Angels of Love *really* want to bring you together with your special person, *they will make it happen!*

That night, as soon as I left Stan's house, I hurried back to my apartment to check the Phoenix telephone book. I had to verify if Mary-Caroline Meadows had really been telling me the truth. Was it really true that Sherry Hansen was living in Phoenix?

It was true. I found the listing: Rev. Sherry Hansen.

I remembered then that in addition to a list of accomplishments as long as my arm, Sherry was also an ordained Protestant minister who had attended the Lutheran School of Theology in Chicago and had later been placed on its staff.

Now all I had to do was to call her. Just pick up the telephone and dial her number. Maybe I could even say that I needed pastoral counseling.

It would take me two weeks to summon the courage to call her. But meanwhile, as I sat alone in my apartment, night after night, I had a lot of time to think about her and the bizarre events of my life that had led me to that particular juncture on my path.

I had first seen Sherry's face after a small-

ish being of multidimensional or otherworldly origin visited me when I was five.
The morning after I had caught sight of the
alien presence at the window of our Iowa
farmhouse, I found a magic circle in our
grove. And while I stood in the midst of its
enchanted perimeter, I could hear beautiful
music and I could see the lovely, smiling face
of a fairy princess who had auburn hair and
unusually large blue-green eyes. At the same
time, I received an inner *knowing* that one
day the princess and I would be together and
accomplish a special kind of work together.

Because I had had a close encounter with
a being that would either be classified as supernatural or extraterrestrial, depending
upon one's cosmological bias, I very early on
understood that our universe is a very much
more wonderful place than even our science
can perhaps imagine and that there truly do
exist "powers and principalities" in the seen
and unseen worlds, just as the Bible informs
us.

My favorite hymn as a child was "Heaven
Is My Home." I seemed to especially relate
to the line, "I'm but a stranger here— Heaven
is my home."

And yet, while recognizing the nonphysical
"heavenly" spark within, I was very keenly
aware of the wonder and the challenge of

being a human being—a child of Earth's dust and of God's breath.

As I reviewed such thoughts in my mind while I sat alone late at night in my apartment, I found it curious that just a few weeks before Mary-Caroline Meadows had brought me the welcome greetings from Sherry, I had experienced a very significant dream about her.

I had been visiting my childhood home in Iowa. My parents' house had suffered a fire which had not destroyed it, but had caused enough damage to encourage them to move into town after a lifetime in the country.

When I came to the spot where the place I'd called "the magic circle" had been, I was saddened to see that only one large tree remained of the once majestic grove of trees and that the highly productive orchard had been plowed under in order to enlarge the tillable area for field crops. I was especially disheartened to see that the lilac bushes which had contained my "secret place" had also been removed.

I was reminded of my experience with the alien entity that had visited our farm when I was a child of five, and I thought longingly of my vision of the beautiful fairy princess.

That night I had a profound dream of Sherry Hansen, the lovely woman who had so briefly entered my office four years before;

and I saw to my complete understanding that she was, as I had suspected upon first seeing her, the human representation of the fairy princess of my childhood vision.

The days went by, and I still had not called Sherry Hansen.

The more I reviewed what I knew about her, the more nervous I became and the more reluctant I was to telephone her.

Although she was an ordained Protestant minister, she had also received national attention as a model, a writer-producer of television commercials, and as a publicist for some of the top acts in show business. If she hadn't developed a fever during a crucial shoot, everyone would know her as the "Excedrin P.M. Girl." If she had not been opposed to cigarette smoking, we would all know her from billboards as the "Marlboro Woman."

She had appeared in small parts in a number of made-for-television movies, but acting was not really her thing. She even turned down an offer from Norman Lear who wanted to build his first feature film around her after he had finished his incredibly popular run with "All in the Family."

Although she had appeared on posters attired in a two-piece swim suit, she rejected lucrative offers from both *Playboy* and *Penthouse* to reveal more.

All these things she had turned down to organize the Butterfly Center for Wholistic Education in Virginia Beach, Virginia, and to serve as a founding member of the Wholistic Healing Board through the Institutes of Health and Education, Washington, D.C.

Sherry had rejected opportunities that others would have "killed for" in order to remain true to her own vision of elevating planetary consciousness.

She was obviously a woman with a mission.

And she was only a telephone number away from me.

Over and over I had rehearsed how I would begin the conversation when I got up the nerve to call her. I decided that I would say that our mutual good friend Mary-Caroline Meadows had relayed her greetings to me at Dr. Caruso's lecture. Then I would apologize for not having called sooner, and I would explain how terribly busy I had been.

But then I got to thinking that a lady might not like to hear that it was another lady who prompted me to call her, so I was uncertain what would be the best ice-breaker.

When I finally did make the call, I found myself speaking to a woman whose very voice transmitted vibrations of love, understanding, and deep wisdom— and I forgot all about mentioning mutual friends or the latest movies or the current trends in local politics or anything, for that matter.

But it still took me another three months to ask her out on a late-night coffee date.

In the meantime, though, our telephone conversations had become increasingly deep, more confessional. We began to talk for hours, releasing veritable floodgates of communication.

One night she called me at one, and we talked until three. That was when we discovered that we were both night people.

Another night she called late to tell me of a remarkable vision that had come to her during a deep meditative experience. Although she found the imagery difficult to express in words, she had seen the two of us exploding into a living pyramid of light.

As she described her vision, I received a clear picture of the two of us surrounded by enormously powerful waves of energy.

I confessed to her that she had always been an enigma and mystery in my life. I admitted that I had flashed on her image a thousand times since we had met briefly so many years before. I even got up the nerve to tell her that I had first become acquainted with her features when I was a small boy— years before she was even born into Earth plane life.

After over three months of telephone conversations, we finally met at midnight for coffee in an all-night restaurant. The impact of seeing her again was almost too much for my senses. In my memories it was her aura, her energy, more than her physical appearance that had enchanted me. In person, however, her auburn-maned beauty and her compellingly large blue-green eyes seemed an incredible bonus.

Both of us wished that the night of endless conversation and perpetually poured cups of coffee would never end, but I had to leave the next morning for Los Angeles to lecture.

The connection had been made, however, and on some deeper level of *knowing* we perceived that it would be forever.

A few days after my return, I received a call from Mary-Caroline Meadows, who in the interim months since our meeting had been away from Phoenix conducting insightful research with dolphins.

After we had chatted for a few minutes, I informed her that I was about to enter a business and research association with a good friend of hers.

"Oh, who is that?" she asked, naturally curious.

"Sherry Hansen."

There were several moments of silence.

"Mary-Caroline?"

"Ah, yes, Brad, I don't think I know anyone named Sherry Hansen."

I was stunned. "Of course you do. The night that we met, you told me that you were bringing me greetings from our mutual dear friend Sherry Hansen."

"Ah, I don't think so."

I was growing a bit impatient. I saw no need for someone failing to remember an incident that had occurred only a few months ago. Especially when it involved people who knew each other well.

"You told me that the two of you were taking a class together. She asked you to say hello to me, to give me her love."

Keeping her voice pleasant, Mary-Caroline said patiently, "Brad, I really do not know anyone named Sherry Hansen, so I could not have promised her that I would bring you greetings from her. Secondly, I have *taught* classes in the Phoenix area, but I have never *taken* a class from anyone in Phoenix."

* * *

I had never mentioned to Sherry the stimulus that had prompted me to call her, but after I had said good-bye to Mary-Caroline, I decided that it was time to raise the issue and to solve the mystery of why Mary-Caroline had denied knowing her.

"I just had a call from your friend Mary-Caroline Meadows," I told Sherry when she answered the telephone at her office.

"My friend, *who?*" she asked.

"Mary-Caroline Meadows. You took a class with her in Phoenix just a few months ago."

Sherry was firm in her response. "I haven't taken a class *with* anyone or *from* anyone since I've been in Phoenix."

"Sher," I said, once more getting a little impatient with the whole business and deciding to come out with it, "it was because you asked Mary-Caroline to greet me at Dr. Caruso's lecture that I even knew you were in Phoenix. It was because of her relaying your message and your wishes of love that I called you."

"That is most interesting, Brad, because I will swear to you on all things that I consider holy that I do *not* know *anyone* by the name of Mary-Caroline Meadows!"

By the time that Sherry and I had finished our conversation that afternoon, I had no question left in my mind: Sherry and Mary-Caroline definitely did not know each other.

And then, for the first time, it became clear to me. Mary-Caroline had been used by some unseen entity who had temporarily entered her in order to bring Sherry and me together. In some remarkable way, the Angels of Love had interacted in the flow of our physical lives. After all these years, they had brought my fairy princess into my arms.

That night in my meditation, I heard the voice of the Light Being that I refer to as my guide speak clearly to my spiritual essence: *"Sherry is the one for whom you have waited for so long. She is truly your destiny."*

We were married near the airport vortex in Sedona, Arizona, by Reverend Jon Terrance Diegel on August 17, 1987, at midnight during the Harmonic Convergence. Jon's wife, Dr. Patricia Rochelle Diegel was in attendance. The Diegels are two of my oldest and dearest friends, who have always been supportive of all aspects of my research. Patricia and Jon accepted Sherry as their sister, as I have been their brother.

Patricia Rochelle, who has performed more than 45,000 psychic readings, advised us that we were not simply two entities coming together as one—we were the equal parts of a whole being.

She also warned us that now that we had

come together, there would be the forces of discord and chaos that would strenuously seek to pull us apart, to break us up, to once again split the single entity in two.

Because I had been scarred emotionally deeper than I believed, I at first experienced some difficulty in being able to accept just how fully and completely Sherry loved me. I had never really believed that I could be loved unconditionally for who and what I truly am.

Soon she helped me to realize that our having been brought together by the Angels of Love had formed the Living Pyramid that she had once described to me. Sherry's quiet wisdom that issues from the vibratory energy of the Oneness enabled her to become the living philosopher's stone that was able to heal my ravaged soul.

About a year after our marriage, we were lecturing in New York City for one of Paul Andrews's Whole Life EXPOs. It was late at night, we were hungry— and nothing seemed to be open except for a few greasy spoon all-night diners. At last we spotted a Chinese restaurant that appeared to be on the third floor of a building not far from our hotel.

There were only two other customers in the

place. One was a man who bore an uncanny resemblance to the actor-comedian, Steve Martin. The other was his companion— Mary-Caroline Meadows.

I had not seen Mary-Caroline for nearly two years. And now—just to set my mind at peace forever— I would soon be able to detect if, in fact, Sherry and Mary-Caroline had ever met each other.

After cheerful introductions, I explained to Mary-Caroline what had occurred in my reality the night that she had sat beside me during Dr. Caruso's demonstration at the Puryears' center. She was astonished, and I suppose it gave all of us a marvelous— yet somewhat eerie feeling— to know without question how subtly the Beings of Light and the Angels of Love can interact with us in our lives.

Mary-Caroline said that she had absolutely no memory of having been "used" in such a manner to achieve such a high purpose, that of bringing two lightworkers together as one. But there was no question that her physical vehicle had been utilized to provoke me into contacting Sherry so that our mission— far too long delayed— could at last move into high gear. She now refers to herself as our Cupid Unaware.

* * *

With each passing day, it becomes clearer to me that Sherry and I have truly become a living pyramid of mind, body, and spirit. We are living crystals of Light and Love, and I know now that there is no power on Earth that can separate us.

Oh, yes, there have been difficult times and dark nights of the soul, but we know that the Angels of Love have blessed us. We have come together to complete a wondrous mission of love and light. We are now linked together in total soul union.

Two

A Snow Angel's
Sweet Intervention

In January of 1972, Gloria Siburg was a freelance writer from Chicago doing a piece for a regional magazine on picturesque vacation spots in remote Midwestern rural areas. She suddenly found herself "in the very midst of the Snow Queen's Kingdom in northern Wisconsin and in the very midst of a raging blizzard."

"Why I thought that I had to set out to do research for the article in the dead of winter was beginning to make no sense at all. I was miles from any town or city, and the snow was coming down so heavy that my windshield wipers were barely able to keep up with it. And then the wind howling through the pine trees on each side of the narrow gravel road began to sound like a starving wolf."

The "oldies" station that Gloria had turned on for cheer and comfort broadcast traveler's advisory warnings after every tune.

"I freely admit that I was becoming very nervous and worried. I knew that my car could get stuck in a snowbank and that I might freeze to death before anyone with road clearing equipment ever found me. Good Lord, I thought, I could be there until the spring thaw!"

As she made her way cautiously around a sharp curve in the road, she thought that she could make out flashing red lights ahead of her. As she drew nearer, she could see a sheriff's patrol car blocking her entrance to a narrow wooden bridge.

An officer got out of the patrol car and, pulling the hood of his parka over his head, walked quickly to Gloria's vehicle.

"Ma'am, you can't keep driving on this road," he told her. "It's completely snow-packed, and it has a lot of dangerous icy spots besides. There is a major blizzard heading this way. You need to get off the roads at once."

He stepped back, glanced at her license plates, saw that her vehicle was registered in Illinois.

"Are you staying anywhere near here?" he asked. His voice was warm and filled with concern.

Gloria fought back tears of desperation and managed to maintain her control when she told him that she was lost and had no idea where she could go for refuge against the storm.

"There's no way that you're going to get very far in this heavy snow," he appraised the situation honestly. "You don't even have snow tires or chains."

Gloria noticed that the deputy appeared to be Native American in physical appearance. That would not be unusual for that particular region of Wisconsin. His eyes were brown and warm, and his manner was courteous and concerned. A shiny metal name plate on his thick winter coat identified him as "Deputy Maleakh," and she decided, judging by the name, that her considerate law enforcement officer was definitely a member of one of the local tribes.

"What can I do, Deputy?" she wanted to know. "I was having trouble driving before I met you. How far is it to the nearest town that would have a motel?"

He shook his head grimly. "At least fifteen miles. And you know that all the rooms are going to be taken by now."

Gloria felt her stomach sink. She had never been in such a desperate situation.

"Tell you what, though," Deputy Maleakh said. "The farmers in these parts are really friendly folk. They would certainly respond to a woman in a crisis situation and be happy to take you in to sit out the storm."

Before Gloria could express her doubts or concerns, the deputy had ordered her to follow him. Under the circumstances, she decided that she really had no choice.

"Deputy Maleakh led me to a farmhouse that was not more than a mile from the bridge where he had stopped me. Thank goodness it was no farther, because my car stalled in a snow bank right in front of the home. The deputy waved good-bye, indicating that I was on my own; and he drove back down the farmer's lane and out on the narrow gravel road. He obviously had to return quickly to the bridge to warn other motorists about the dangerous road conditions ahead."

A beautiful blonde girl of about eleven answered her desperate knock at the door and, without hesitation, helped Gloria inside.

"Her father, she said as she poured me a cup of steaming hot coffee, was outside seeing to the livestock's safety. There was a big storm coming, she told me with great solemnity. We could be snowbound for days."

Gloria admitted that her account would go on to read like a romance novel.

"Suffice it to say that an Angel of Love had directed me to the love of my life, Mike Emerick. When he came into the kitchen of the farmhouse all red-faced and covered with snow, my heart felt cupid's arrow hit a bull's-eye! To my everlasting shame, I felt my pulse quicken when I learned that his wife Martha had passed away two years ago, leaving him on the farm with only his daughter Melanie."

The next four days and nights were almost as if they had been taken from the pages of a turn-of-the-century account of being snow-bound in the country. They played cards, popped corn, listened to records, and watched old movies late at night on television.

"And even though I could see, feel, and *know* that Mike felt a mutual attraction to me, we were exceedingly discreet for Melanie's sake."

The telephone lines had been down for the first couple of days of Gloria's stay with the Emericks, but as soon as she got a dial tone, she told Mike that she wanted to thank Deputy Maleakh for his courtesy and for saving her life— not to mention connecting her with the man of her dreams.

"That's when Mike told me that he knew of no one named Maleakh in the Sheriff's department. Mike had lived there all of his life and knew everyone on the staff.

"Theorizing that someone unknown to Mike and someone very new to the region might have joined the department, I called the Sheriff and inquired about Deputy Maleakh. With a deep chuckle, he confirmed what Mike had said, then asked if this were some kind of joke.

"So at that time, I was left completely baffled as to the true identity of the Good Samaritan who had saved my life and who had brought me together with Mike."

Although Gloria had to return to Chicago, she and Mike were soon running up huge long-distance telephone bills and writing lengthy love letters to one another. When she visited Mike and Melanie in early spring, she found the area to be breathtakingly beautiful.

She had always been a big-city girl, but the natural Earth Mother beauty of rural northern Wisconsin was becoming an ever-stronger lure. And the quiet of a country farmhouse would be an ideal place to write.

It wasn't until she and Mike had decided to be married that Gloria told her priest about the remarkable circumstances with the nonexistent Deputy Maleakh that had brought her together with the love of her life.

"Father Donlon looked at me quizzically and then broke out into a broad smile.

" 'Gloria,' he said, 'your marriage is going to be truly blessed. *Maleakh* is the Hebrew word that explains what angels are, the messengers of God. And it just so happened that that particular angelic messenger was also a cupid!' "

Three

Reunion with
His Heavenly Classmate

When Robert Ferrin was seven years old, he had a near-death experience when he almost died after being struck by an automobile. As sometimes occurs, young Bob was returned to life with accelerated paranormal abilities.

"During my out-of-body journey to higher dimensions, I encountered a beautiful angel of light who told me that he was my guardian angel who would always be with me. I was told that it was not yet my time to remain in the heavenly realms, so I was returned to my battered little body in the hospital."

But it wasn't long before little Bobby noticed that he could "hear" the unspoken thoughts of others.

"This can be very disconcerting to a seven-year-old. I was really frightened at first, but I soon learned to be very discreet about my new ability.

"Then, when I was eleven or so, I discovered that I was also picking up the emotional vibrations of others. This really proved to be very difficult for me, because it took me quite a while to be truly aware of what was taking place."

One night, alone in his room, Bob was wondering what was happening to him, and his angel guide manifested before him in a glowing envelope of light.

"He told me that I was to serve as a Golden Light of Peace and Love. He said that while others around me might be spinning around in emotional and mental turmoil, I was to transmit a loving energy of tranquility and balance.

"My angel warned me that this would not be an easy thing to accomplish on the Earth plane. He said that I would have to practice diligently to achieve mental and emotional harmony.

"He certainly was correct, for I failed often

in my attempts to be a kind of emotional balancer. Especially during those teenage years."

When he was thirteen or fourteen, Bob remembers being taken by his angel in dreams to a beautiful golden temple on some dimension of reality.

"I was taught many awesome and beautiful things in this temple by a hooded teacher, who never quite revealed his face. Everything was explained to me in terms of energy and vibrational patterns. I was told that there were many different levels of reality. As a human, I could only see one level at a time. As a multidimensional being, I could perceive many different levels at the same time.

"Good and evil, as we humans understood the concepts, did not truly exist. There were various levels of positive and negative energies, and whether we performed acts of 'good' or 'evil' depended upon our resonance to particular vibrational levels. Nothing would be negative (evil) forever. All energies would eventually be positive and pure and One."

One night when he was sixteen, as he tried his best to absorb these higher-level teachings in some other dimension of reality, he was suddenly able to see more of the celestial environment than ever before; and he could clearly see other human students seated around him. Almost all of the members of the class were teenagers, like himself.

"When I awakened the next morning, one powerful thought reverberated within my consciousness mind: I was not alone. There were others like me!"

Bob remembered one girl in particular—a lovely young woman of about his age who had reddish-brown hair and bright blue-green eyes. He vowed then that some day he would find her.

At the same time that he was feeling very acutely alone among his friends and classmates in Cincinnati, Ohio, he found that he was becoming increasingly popular. He overheard teachers and his peers alike talking about his "charisma," the "optimistic energy he exuded," the "positive nature" he always displayed.

"You just feel like you want to be around him as much as you can, don't you?" he heard one of the varsity cheerleaders saying to a group of her friends as he walked by them on the way to class one day. "There's something about Bob that just makes you feel good."

Bob became active in as many sports and

extracurricular activities as his time would permit. He was better at some pursuits than others, of course, but that never seemed to bother him. He told his friends not to be afraid to try different projects and activities, because there was really no such thing as failure.

"There is only the state of being and the opportunity for growth and love," he said.

"Love? Even in football, when you're supposed to smash the bum on the opposing team?" a buddy asked to the amusement of the other guys in the locker room.

"Even then," Bob answered with an indulgent smile.

Bob dated only to fulfill social obligations at those events on the high school calendar when it seemed appropriate to do so, but he had no special feelings for any of the girls he escorted to those special occasions. He knew that somewhere one of his fellow classmates in the Angelic Dream School was waiting for him to arrive.

"For a while there, I thought she would never show up," Robert said in his account of his interaction with the Angels of Love. "And then one day when I was twenty-nine, something caused me to turn around to face the person behind me at a bus stop—and there she was. Reddish-brown hair, bright blue-green eyes, the same intense look that I remembered from those night classes when I was a teenager."

Although Robert was normally a reserved, self-contained kind of fellow, he knew that this was the time to put all that behind him and to seize the moment.

"I know you from somewhere," he said. "Somewhere really important. Almost heavenly, you could say."

She snapped out of her reverie, startled by the stranger speaking to her. He could read her expressions easily. She was almost ready to deal harshly with some fresh, male chauvinist on the street, but after she actually took a focused look at him, she frowned, then offered him a friendly smile.

"Why . . . why, yes," she laughed. "I believe that I do know you from . . . *somewhere*. You are also very familiar to me. Was it high school?"

"You from Cincinnati?"

"No. New York City. I'm here on business for my company. I went to high school in a small town outside of Buffalo."

"Scratch high school then," Robert said. "I'm from Cincinnati. My name is Robert Ferrin. Shouldn't we get off the street corner and go somewhere nice, have a cup of coffee, maybe a little lunch, and talk about it?"

She said that her name was Sandra Yarnell, and she agreed that they should do exactly that.

When he helped her off with her coat at the small, quiet restaurant he had selected for its lack of clientele at that particular hour of the day, he noticed that she wore a small, golden angel on a chain around her neck.

"Do you believe in angels?" he asked her.

"Yes, most definitely."

"Have you ever seen one?"

Sandra looked in his eyes for a long, silent moment as they were being seated at a small table in the back. "Yes," she answered. "As a matter of fact, I have."

She folded her napkin neatly in her lap. When she looked up again, she had tears in her eyes. "And so have you, haven't you, Robert?"

A memory of having seen Robert at their angelic classroom in another dimension had suddenly returned to Sandra, and she reached for his hand.

"I've been waiting for you . . . hoping for you . . . looking for you since I was sixteen," he told her.

"And I for you," she said softly, blinking back new tears.

* * *

"I had always known that she was out there waiting for me somewhere," Robert Ferrin concluded his report. "I had always known that I was not alone, that there were other angelically tutored kids out there who had now matured and were doing what they could to spread love and light to all the world.

"Sandra and I totally readjusted our present life patterns to accommodate each other. We now live and work in the region near Carmel, California, and we conduct workshops and seminars in creating a loving reality in a world of chaos."

Four

An Angelic Love Story

Jonathan Scordo of Gainesville, Florida, was a sickly child who suffered from severe allergic reactions to almost everything.

"My sole form of solace came from an angel who always appeared to me as a cowled figure, much like that of a monk. His voice was gentle, soothing, and his words were filled with wisdom and love. He said that his name was Jedidiah."

Jonathan told me that he had first met his angel when he was only five years old.

"I started to fall down the stairway, and someone reached out and pulled me back to a sitting position on the landing. I looked up to see this bearded man bending over and smiling at me.

"My older sister, Sarah, who was supposed to be baby-sitting me, saw me totter at the top of the steps, start to topple, then appear to fly backward to the landing. 'You must have a guardian angel!' she exclaimed in her twelve-year-old wisdom."

When Jonathan was nine, he tripped into the fireplace and burned his left forearm terribly.

"The skin appeared charred and blistered. While Father called the doctor, Mom carried me to my room and put wet cloths on the burned area. I remember the pain was excruciating.

"When Mom stepped out of the room to get some fresh cloths, Jedidiah appeared and placed the forefinger of his right hand on my burned forearm. He simply traced a straight line with his finger— and the charred area of flesh was immediately transformed back into healthy skin."

The family doctor was a personal friend of Jonathan's father, but he was still very upset over being called out on a rainy night for nothing.

"My parents protested that I had been badly burned and that they had both seen me fall into the fireplace and had both seen the area of blackened flesh. After the angry physician had departed, my sister Sarah— who was by then an exceedingly wise sixteen-year-old— told my parents quite simply and directly that 'his angel just worked another miracle, that's all.' "

When he himself turned sixteen, Jonathan was startled one night to see a strange manifestation of a greenish, glowing ball of light that appeared in his bedroom shortly after he had finished meditating.

"The glowing object just seemed to shoot around my room at great speed, yet never hitting a wall, any of the furniture, or the ceiling.

"And then suddenly it seemed as though my spiritual essence was out of my body and racing along beside the glowing ball!

"This remains one of the most exhilarating experiences that I have ever had— zipping around the room like an accelerated ping-pong ball that never had to touch anything in order to bounce.

"And then my spiritual essence and the glowing ball seemed to soar up through the ceiling and upward into the dark night sky. We seemed to dance among the stars. The feeling was absolutely ecstatic!"

After that liberating experience, Jonathan found that all of his debilitating allergies had left him. It was as if he had left his cocoon of illness and pain and emerged as a butterfly, free of blights and blemishes.

"I still had the occasional sinus headache, but all in all, I felt wonderful. I knew that it was Jedidiah, my guardian angel, who had assumed the form of the mysterious glowing ball to set my physical body free of all those restrictive illnesses and allergies."

When Jonathan met Elizabeth Carley in 1985, she was a twenty-year-old waitress who was hoping to get the right audition with the right recording executive and emerge as a singing superstar.

Jonathan was a twenty-eight-year-old high-school sociology teacher and guidance counselor, who was popular and well-liked by his students.

"Jedidiah would often enter my consciousness and speak through me to the students. Of course, neither they nor my superiors on the staff knew that I was channeling an angel during some of my guidance sessions. Jedidiah had a knack for saying what people *needed* to hear, rather than what they *wanted* to hear, so while some of the students might be stung by his initial comments, the truth of his counsel always rang true. And best of all, it always seemed to help them."

Elizabeth came to Jonathan's table to take his order, and she was startled when he suddenly reached up and gently took the order pad from her hands and placed her left hand in his right.

"You have a great deal of talent, young lady. Why did you leave college?" he asked her.

In her version of their meeting, Elizabeth laughed and told me that she was at first offended. She assumed he was just some wise guy trying to get fresh with her.

"But there was something about his voice and his bright blue eyes that made me stop and listen to him. And his touch—it was soothing and electrical at the same time!"

Elizabeth asked who he was. Had they met before?

"We've only met before on the inner planes," Jonathan smiled in response to her question. "I think our guardian angels know each other."

Elizabeth thought that she had encountered a religious freak or a guy with the most original line she had ever heard.

"You have a great talent for music," Jonathan was telling her, "but you have misdirected it with a false dream. You should go back to college and be a music teacher. You would be such a good teacher."

Elizabeth said that her first impulse was to tell the nosy customer that he had some nerve trying to tell her what to do, and to mind his own business.

"But there was something about his manner that wasn't mean-spirited or fresh or smart-alecky. He just seemed to be saying these things as matter-of-factly as if he were reading the stock reports in the newspaper."

She told him that she had to take his order. The boss didn't allow the waitresses to stand around and talk to the customers.

Jonathan nodded and ordered the special.

When Elizabeth got off work in an hour, Jonathan was still there.

She collected the money for his bill, then whispered that she would like to talk to him when she got off work in a couple of minutes.

"I knew that the guy could have been some nut or serial killer or something. I had never seen him in there before, after all. But there was something about his calm, yet pointed, manner of speaking that seemed so kind and loving. I mean loving in a universal way. And I had to find out how he could know so much about me!"

Jonathan offered his car as a place to sit

and talk, but the cautious Elizabeth pointed out her battered old four-door Chevrolet in the parking lot and suggested that they just ride around for a while. She figured that if they were in her car and she was at the wheel, she would have a bit more control over the situation than if she were a passenger in his car. That was if he proved to be some kind of nut or something, that is.

The two of them talked until nearly dawn. They soon abandoned the woebegone Chevy and found an all-night diner in which they could share comments, ideas, and concepts with only the occasional interruption of a tired waitress refilling their coffee cups.

"Elizabeth didn't know it at the time, of course, but I let Jedidiah do most of the talking," Jonathan said. "It was he who convinced her to go back to college."

Elizabeth was astonished by the entire evening. "I felt as if I were dreaming. Not only is this complete stranger telling me what an illusion a career as a nightclub singer would be for me to pursue, but he is praising my ability to become a serious singer and teacher of voice. What is more, he is offering to help finance my return to college!"

When Elizabeth protested such an offer,

Jonathan shrugged and laughed away her objections.

He told her that he was a single man living inexpensively in a studio apartment. He had no expensive hobbies, no extravagant vices, no lavish tastes.

"No girlfriend?" Elizabeth wanted to know.

Jonathan smiled at her over the rim of his coffee cup. "I have many girl *friends*. But no one serious if that's what you mean."

It was still all too much for Elizabeth to consider in such a brief time.

"Look at it this way," Jonathan argued. "I am investing in your future. I have been very blessed in my life. The angelic law of the universe says that when one has been blessed, it is the divine obligation of that person to bless another. One day it will be your obligation to pass the blessing on."

Elizabeth agreed that he had a lovely philosophy, but he was talking about more than a blessing. He was talking about money.

"Oh, very well then," Jonathan sighed, "if you are so concerned about the money, some day you can pay me back as you are able. We'll call it a loan for now."

"A loan sounds better," Elizabeth nodded.

"Better than a blessing?" Jonathan wondered at her process of evaluation. "Extraordinary."

"How is it you know so much about blessings and angels?" she asked him.

And then, for the next two hours, Jonathan told her all about Jedidiah, his angelic mentor.

By the time that the two of them left the all-night diner at 5:15 A.M., they had agreed to a plan regarding Jonathan's pledge to enable Elizabeth to complete her final year and a half at college.

"I drove Jonathan back to the restaurant parking lot so he could get into his car and dash home to his apartment to shower and shave before he was to be at school by 8:00. I knew then, of course, that I had met the most extraordinary man in the western hemisphere— if not the entire world. I also knew that I had fallen in love in one night."

Jonathan felt completely exhilarated that entire day at school— even though he had not been able to capture one wink of sleep.

"That magical evening had brought me something far more invigorating than sleep. The moment that I had walked into that restaurant at what I thought was completely at random, Jedidiah whispered in my ear that my destiny would soon be at my side. The moment I looked into Elizabeth's eyes, I felt as if I was once again that sixteen-year-old boy soaring through the stars with my angelic mentor. After that, I just permitted Jedidiah to do all my talking for me."

Elizabeth said that Jonathan was at all times the perfect gentleman during the next two years.

"I am positive that I kissed him first. And that was after we had met for coffee and dinner half a dozen times.

"He still hung back quite a distance until I was once again well into the flow of college classes, then we began to see each other regularly. I still kept a part-time job at the restaurant, and Jonathan, of course, had his teaching and counseling assignments."

However, neither of them was very surprised when Jedidiah recommended to Jonathan that he present Elizabeth with an engagement ring on her graduation day.

Since 1988, Elizabeth and Jonathan have been teaching in the same Georgia high school, being of service and counsel to their students and their community.

Five

Drawn Together
in Spirit

Anastasia and Jon Marc Hammer, the co-directors of Heartlight Ministries of Santa Fe, New Mexico, a non-profit, educational entity dedicated to personal and planetary healing, came together in a way which clearly demonstrates the helping hand of guides that often seem to know our destiny more clearly than we do. But they affirm that their story tells us more: That soulmates come together for very specific purposes— purposes which often find their origins in other times and places.

* * *

"Imagine if you will," they wrote in their account of their unusual series of experiences, "what happened to Jon Marc one incredible morning in 1987. He had been rushing about his home in the State of Washington, doing all the usual things he did to get himself out the door and to his office.

"Suddenly, he heard a voice that seemed to come from everywhere. The voice spoke with calm certainty, great authority, and a depth of love.

"Along with the voice, Jon Marc felt embraced by waves of an incredibly peaceful, nurturing energy— unlike anything he had ever known.

"The voice said calmly: *'Please sit and meditate.'* "

Without further thought concerning his busy schedule, Jon Marc put his briefcase down, proceeded to the couch, closed his eyes, and went within. As his mind became quiet, a light seemed to appear in the distance, growing brighter as it moved toward him. The waves of energy that he had felt earlier were now lifting him higher and higher into the light itself.

"Then a form of someone began to appear," Jon Marc said. "It was the form of someone a part of me knew beyond all doubt. He came so close that I could feel him merge with me. He shared many things, including his name. It is a name with which millions are familiar.

" *'I am Jeshua, whom the world knows as Jesus,'* he told me."

A part of Jon Marc knew then that his life had taken an abrupt turn, a turn that somewhere in the sleeping corners of his mind, he *knew* had long ago been agreed upon.

That was how Jon Marc came to find himself serving as both channel and author, sharing the message of Jeshua with people across the country.

"But I had no way of knowing that Jeshua was also working behind the scenes with someone else who was coming to a major place of awakening— someone I would come to recognize more deeply than anyone I had ever encountered."

Anastasia had been living a normal life in Chico, California. Like Jon Marc, she was in a "comfortable" relationship, one based on all the "right" reasons. But something was beginning to brew within her. There was a longing welling up within her heart.

"I remember one day in particular," she said. "My husband had gone off to work, and I had sat down on the couch. As I looked around me, everything seemed so *good!* Nice house, creature comforts, a wonderful dog, friends. But something was beginning to call me from somewhere in my soul. I lit some candles and began to meditate, gazing into a mirror in front of me."

What began to unfold was something that Anastasia could never have predicted.

"All of a sudden, I began to sob uncontrollably— deep convulsions of tears that came from my very core.

"The pain became so intense that I confess to thoughts of just wanting to die, to leave the planet."

Anastasia's thinking mind could make no sense out of what had happened to her.

"I called a friend, a nationally known psychic, who told me that I was beginning a major process of transformation, that the tears were nothing to worry about.

"Later, feeling exhausted, I went to bed and fell quickly to sleep."

But that particular night's sleep would prove to be very different from all others.

About 2:00 A.M., Anastasia felt nudged awake. When she sat up, her whole body began to tremble, to vibrate with an amazingly gentle and loving energy.

She heard a thought within her mind: *Sit and meditate.*

"When I arranged myself before the mirror,

I was shocked to see that it was not my own face staring back at me. It was the face of someone for whom I had felt great fondness throughout my life. I had tucked this unexplainable fondness safely in the closet of my mind, for it had always seemed as though the world would not understand my sense of *knowing* this nonphysical friend. In the mirror was the face of Jeshua."

Anastasia said that she remembers clearly being transported to a timeless, loving space, immersed in light and love that swept away a fog that had been covering her awareness.

"I sensed that my purpose for coming to the planet was being remembered and that Jeshua was silently confirming something of importance to me. The anguish was gone, and I felt deeply at peace."

But things were only beginning. Over the next several months, both Jon Marc and Anastasia began to have dreams that were very different in quality— dreams that left each of them feeling that something was stirring just out of sight of their surface consciousness.

"I began having dreams of a woman with long blond hair and eyes filled with light coming toward me," Jon Marc said. "Each time I beheld this woman, I clearly felt my heart stirring in ways that I had never before experienced.

"Interestingly, I eventually recalled this dream as the same one that had repeated itself to me at the age of twelve. Since I had been unable to understand their meaning then, the dreams had gradually been forgotten."

In her series of unusual dreams, Anastasia was envisioning a man— a man who was definitely *not* the man with whom she was currently in a relationship.

"The energy that I felt in my heart during the dreams was unlike anything I could imagine," she recalled. "I was afraid to share them with anyone. How would I be able to describe something so hauntingly familiar that generated such a profound sense of oneness— yet it was not connected to anyone I knew. Especially not the man I was sleeping next to!"

In the coming weeks— during meditation or being nudged awake from sleep— Anastasia would suddenly see the image of this man hovering near her for just a moment. And each time the experience would always elicit the same deep feelings of ancient familiarity.

* * *

Meanwhile, Jon Marc would find himself in the midst of his normal daily activities and he would suddenly feel as though his heart was about to explode out of his chest. At the same time, he would feel immersed in warmth and in light. He, too, kept such matters to himself.

One day a friend of Jon Marc's expressed an intuitive notion that he should visit Chico, California, and share his work with Jeshua there.

The words struck him like a bolt of lightning, and he felt resistant to the idea. "Where the heck is Chico? I don't know anyone there!"

But his friend was quite insistent and said that she would make some telephone calls to get an evening group set up for his visit. Grudgingly, Jon Marc agreed to go.

At the same time, Anastasia was enjoying a vacation in the Teton Mountains.

"As was my habit," she said, "I got up one morning and found a quiet spot to meditate. As I simply enjoyed being with Mother Earth, I relaxed very quickly into a quiet space.

"Suddenly an image of Jeshua appeared in my mind, and I was immediately aware of the thought: *Go home now!* So certain and clear was the message that I awakened my partner and told him matter-of-factly that we were cutting our vacation short. Oddly, he complied without a word of objection."

When she arrived home, Anastasia had a message on her answering machine from her yoga teacher, who advised her that some fellow was coming from the State of Washington, and that he channeled Jesus. Would she like to go?

"Every cell in my body tingled," Anastasia remembered. "Of course I wanted to go. I was sure that this was why Jeshua had appeared to me in the Tetons.

"I had always pooh-poohed channeling, yet as the time for the meeting drew near, my heart was racing. At first I thought that I should call everyone in my meditation group to attend the session— but a little voice kept saying, 'No, this is for you.'"

Anastasia recalled that on her way out of the door of her home, her partner remarked, "Be sure the guy is not a charlatan!"

Without a second's hesitation, she had replied that she would know the moment she walked into the place whether or not the man was genuine.

Later, she would wonder where these words, spoken with such certainty, had come from.

When she did enter the room where the

event was being held, she saw a number of
people milling about chatting. Then her eyes
riveted on a man in the midst of the crowd.

"My whole being stopped," she said. "I felt
a *whoosh* of energy. The man turned and
looked at me, and just as quickly turned away
again. There was such an immediate knowing.

"I muttered something to my friend who
had come with me, but I was unaware at the
time that I had said anything at all.

"I do remember saying, 'There is the most
beautiful being I have ever known.' And then
I mumbled that I had probably better sit
down before I fell down."

As the evening progressed, Anastasia felt
the familiar waves of loving energy that she
had experienced on those occasions when
Jeshua had appeared to her.

"I did not see Jon Marc's physical form at
all. It was more like light—and within the
light there appeared kaleidoscopic images of
various persons from different time frames.
Each one felt completely familiar. I sensed
that I was in a new place of awareness. The
floodgates had opened—nothing would ever
be quite the same."

Jon Marc stated that his responses toward
Anastasia were a bit slower.

"When I felt that whoosh of energy and turned to see her, my breath stopped. I wanted to leave the room! I was in a relationship that was quite comfortable, and I did not want to feel anything that would rock the boat."

The next day, Anastasia came for a private session with Jon Marc.

"It was like a homecoming, touching the deepest part of my heart," she recalled. "And it was very clear that Jeshua knew me completely."

Near the end of the session, she asked Jeshua when she would know what part, if any, she had to play in the work that was unfolding with him.

Jeshua asked her to "tune in" and perceive the answer.

"In ninety days," Anastasia said.

Jeshua told her that her response was accurate.

Jon Marc returned to his home in Washington, but something had begun to move within him. Try as he might, he could not prevent feelings of oneness with Anastasia from arising within his very essence. Somehow his coming together with her seemed so inevitable.

As things turned out, it was exactly ninety days later when Jon Marc returned to Chico. And now the floodgates would open completely for Anastasia and him.

After Jon Marc's initial visit to Chico, Anastasia had a powerful dream of Jon Marc and her walking in a local park.

"He put his arm around my waist in a friendly sort of way. We looked at each other—and all the veils blocking recognition of our union dissolved away.

"When I awoke from the dream, I cried deeply and convinced myself that I had surely created a fantasy in my mind."

One day after he had returned to Chico for another evening event and a few days of private readings, Jon Marc was passing some free time watching Anastasia play with her German shepherd, Schatzie.

"I suddenly heard a voice that instructed me to *'pay attention,'*" Jon Marc said. "Then it felt as though fingers were prying open my forehead. I began to see images of lifetime after lifetime in which Anastasia and I had been together. The images stretched back through time and finally disappeared into a radiant golden light."

He excused himself politely and went off to bed where he begged Jeshua to help him understand what had just occurred.

"All Jeshua would say was that it was important for me to allow myself to feel everything deeply— and that there would be a time when we would be able to discuss it."

The very next day, Anastasia's precognitive dream played itself out exactly as she had experienced it.

On their walk in the park, Jon Marc put his arm around her waist, and they began to share openly all those things which they had been individually experiencing.

They were so sure of their destiny together, neither of them was surprised when Jon Marc asked, "Will you be moving to Washington, or will I move to Chico?" Anastasia simply replied, "I will move to Washington."

In retrospect, Anastasia commented that it was all quite matter-of-fact.

"It was just a given. It wasn't a walk in the park filled with romanticism. We simply _knew_ in the deepest place in our shared heart that we were to be together— and that the time had finally come."

* * *

When Jon Marc flew home to Washington, it was his turn for tears.

"I sobbed all the way home, tears flowing without shame. It felt as if a dam had burst, as though the purpose of my life was just beginning."

Jon Marc felt that he needed some really specific answers, so he went to the mountain to meditate, to try to get to the bottom of all that had happened to him.

"Every time that I asked Jeshua for help, all that he would say was that it was important for me to continue to feel everything deeply— and that at the proper time, we would be able to talk about it."

Jon Marc hiked by moonlight to a favorite hot spring— only to discover someone else there.

As he turned to leave, he heard Jeshua say, "Stay and listen."

At that same moment, the man in the hot spring noticed Jon Marc and asked him to join him in the pool.

"He began sharing that something had compelled him to drive four hours to this place. On the way, he began to think about the life of Jesus, and he had felt a longing to be closer to him.

"Then he casually said that he had been gay all of his life, but that a few months ago, a woman had walked into his shop and they had experienced an instant recognition. And now they were married! He asked if I had ever heard about soul mates.

"It was clear why I was supposed to be in that hot spring at just that time."

Back in his tent, Jon Marc sat in meditation, determined to get to the bottom of all the incredible things that had been happening to him. As he went deeper into all that had unfolded, he was finally forced to see that he, too, had met his soulmate— a term that previously he had always brushed aside.

Once he had achieved that realization, he immediately felt Jeshua's presence. *"Now, we can begin to talk about these things!"*

Jeshua told Jon Marc that he was now at a major crossroads in his present life experience.

"He explained that I was undergoing an initiation of sorts, and the conflict that I was feeling was between my head and my heart and between the pressures of how the world thinks and what the soul knows. He concluded by saying that it should be abundantly clear to me after those several years with him that he would advocate the wisdom of the soul which speaks to us through the heart."

One week later, a large group of people had gathered in Seattle to hear Jeshua's message. At the end of the evening, after everyone had left, a woman named Karen came back inside and asked to speak privately with Jon Marc.

"Do you remember when I had a private session with Jeshua about seven months ago?" she asked him.

"Yes," Jon Marc replied. "Vaguely."

"Well," she continued, "Jeshua asked if I would do him a favor—to which I quickly agreed. He asked that I deliver a message to you. When I asked him *when* I should do this, he said, 'Fear not. You will know beyond doubt.'

"Just as I was getting into my car tonight to go home, I felt this very strong nudge, and I heard a voice saying that the time was now. I tried to ignore it, but it grew insistent.

"The message is, *Trust your heart.*'"

The resistance in Jon Marc melted away when he recognized the masterful weaving of guidance that Jeshua had given him.

He cried and hugged Karen and told her that she had no idea of the blessing that she had just bestowed upon him.

Somewhat puzzled, Karen turned and walked back to her car.

Back in Chico, Anastasia remembered that she wasn't "quite finished, either." She had called two very good psychics for confirmation.

"Both of them said that they saw our soul-strands going back into infinity.

"I was told by one that she could clearly see Jesus and he was sharing with her that his blessings were upon our union and that our souls had long ago signed the 'contract' to be always together."

Within a month, the two of them had walked through their personal ordeal by fire and were together.

They knew little about one another's personality, but they considered such matters rather insignificant. Finally the world made sense to them.

They had discovered a safety with each other, a safety that has allowed each to heal deeply all "unfinished business."

Through their Heartlight Ministries, Marc and Anastasia present workshops, classes, seminars, and extended retreats around the country. The essential goal of their work is to assist others to open their hearts, empower their lives, and to recognize themselves as the radiant lights they are. Their work with those requesting help with relationships is called "Sacred Intimacy."

Kendra Press, the publishing branch of Heartlight Ministries, distributes the teachings of Jeshua in communion with Jon Marc. Current titles include *The Jeshua Letters* and *The Way of the Servant*.

"We feel that we are being asked to help facilitate a new model of relationship, one based on a new paradigm of an androgynous union committed to mutual empowerment and planetary healing," Anastasia and Jon Marc told me.

"It is time to let go of the old model of relationships, which are often created from the ego's attempt to find comfort and security from the world— rather than listening to the still, small voice within. While at first it may be frightening to pay heed to that voice, it will make all the difference, as evidenced by our personal stories.

"Many people ask us how they may find that special someone, and our answer is always the same:

"When we came together, we were not seeking each other. We feel that our experiences started to unfold naturally, because on some unseen level we were ready and willing to be together.

"Know that you are whole now— and put your focus on healing your sense of separation from God.

"When you grasp the awareness that you are complete *now*, the universe is able to mirror that awareness back to you in the form of a relationship. When it is time, you simply won't be able to prevent such a union from occurring.

"Or as our friend and teacher Jeshua once put it: 'Seek ye first the kingdom, and all these things will be added unto you.'"

Part Two

Angels of Love: Guardians from Beyond

Six

Listen to Your Soul

Dave Ragan, who now lives in a medium-sized city in Missouri, wrote to my office to tell of the angel that first manifested in his presence when he was a child of five.

"I will never forget the image of the beautiful entity when I was playing in the woods near our home in Idaho. I couldn't really tell if the angel was male or female, but the voice that I heard inside my head seemed to be a bit more feminine. It was soft and gentle, kind of like hearing sweet music being played on a harp.

"The angel said that it would always be with me, guiding me, looking after me. I remember being really afraid, but she told me to have no fear. She said that she loved me."

The angel contacted Dave several times throughout his childhood.

"The second time, I didn't see her, but I definitely heard her voice warning me not to enter a cave. I remember that I thought, 'why not?' because I had seen some older boys crawl into the cave a few weeks before. Then I got a mental image of a rattlesnake, and I pulled out right away. A few days later, a hunter told my father that he had shot the 'granddaddy of all rattlesnakes' near that same cave."

A couple of times after that, Dave thought that he might have caught a glimpse of his guardian angel, but as the years went by, he had to be contented with only the sound of her sweet, musical voice speaking to him inside his head.

"A rather strange aspect to my story is that my family was not particularly religious. We went to church on most of the religious holidays, but not too much more. I remember one exasperated minister accusing my father of being a 'Christmas Christian.' So why I had this constant interaction with an angel was always rather puzzling to me. I mean, it wasn't as if I had done anything to deserve it."

* * *

Dave had gone steady with a girl during his senior year in high school.

"She was getting really serious, and she was quite upset when we went to different colleges. We wrote for a time and carried on a long-distance romance for most of the first semester, but my feelings for her cooled, and during the holiday break, I told her that I thought we should start seeing other people.

"I had expected a few tears, but she really tore into me. She said a lot of personal things that really hurt my feelings. I left her place feeling terribly confused, wondering if I had done the right thing. But then I heard my angel's voice clear as could be inside my head: *'Don't be disturbed. Don't despair. She is not the one with whom you'll spend your life.'* "

Dave began to get serious toward the end of his junior year in college when he actually bought an engagement ring for a stunning, dark-haired girl from Montana.

"She was vivacious, really lovely, and filled with seemingly inexhaustible energy. And when I went home with her during one vacation break to meet her parents, I saw that her daddy owned a very large spread of ranchland. She didn't seem to be in any hurry to settle down, but I had decided that

I didn't want to take any chances of her getting away from me.

"I was about to pop the question. I had even memorized a couple verses of some really romantic poetry to help me create the most dramatic effect when I brought out the diamond ring after a lavish dinner at an expensive restaurant.

"Although it does seem amusing in retrospect, my angel whispered to me right after I had ordered dessert and just before I brought out the engagement ring. *This would be a terrible mistake that you would always regret. She is not the one who will make a suitable life partner for you.'*

"With those words ringing inside my head, the night of nights became simply a marvelous dinner at a fine restaurant.

"About a week later, she broke our date to go to the movies, pleading a bad head cold and a touch of the flu. But later that evening my roommate and I saw her dancing with one of the big men on campus, a rich jerk who belonged to one of the other fraternities.

"That's when my buddy leveled with me and told me that he had heard through the rumor mill that she had been two-timing me for months. He had not wanted to hurt my feelings until he had some definite proof that she was messing around behind my back.

"I really surprised my roommate when I

said I wanted to stop by the chapel before I went back to our apartment. He left me alone, thinking that I must really be broken up. Well, of course, I was hurt and upset. But what I really wanted to do was to thank my guardian angel for saving me from making a very bad mistake.

"The jeweler was decent enough to take the ring back—but he did hold back a little over a hundred dollars 'for his trouble.' But I considered that I was still money ahead. Divorces are a lot more expensive than engagement rings."

Dave continued to date—perhaps much more cautiously—always looking forward to the day when the sweet, melodic voice of his angel would give him the green light for a permanent relationship.

It didn't happen for him until he was nearly thirty and becoming quite successful as a real estate salesman.

"Tina Mattes, a very attractive young widow of twenty-eight with two small children—a boy and a girl—stopped by my office to discuss the various issues involved in listing her house with my agency. She lived in an exclusive part of the city, she explained, and because her husband had been killed in an automobile accident the year before, she did not feel that she could afford to keep up the mortgage payments on such a large house.

Unfortunately, her husband, Brian Mattes, had been woefully underinsured; and now she bravely accepted her responsibility to make the necessary adjustments in lifestyle in order to protect the future welfare of her children.

"I was quite astonished when my angel spoke up loud and clear inside my head: *This is the one. She is the one for you. She is the one selected as your helpmate on your lifepath.*'"

That night, after work, Dave sat quietly in the darkness of his apartment and asked his angel aloud if she had truly meant what she had said about the young widow.

The answering voice seemed to issue from all around him: *"She is truly the one for you. She is the one for whom we have waited."*

"I don't mean to sound insensitive," Dave apologized to his unseen guide, "but the lady has two children. I feel somewhat awkward saying this, but I think it would be difficult for me to start a marriage with two kids already there. I mean, I think I would need some time to get adjusted to married life before I could deal with kids."

"It is part of your destiny to be a father. You need such life experiences for the good and the gaining of your Soul."

Dave protested that he was not saying that

he did not wish to have children. He felt only that he would need some time to prepare mentally and emotionally for fatherhood.

"You do not have the proper seed to father children of your own. The only children who will grace your home will be those given to you by another."

Dave puzzled over his angel's words, but she would speak to him no more that night.

The next morning he had an appointment with Tina Mattes at her home for the purpose of writing up a complete listing of the qualities and advantages that her residence might offer a prospective buyer.

"I arrived at ten in the morning—and by three I hadn't even thought of my one o'clock luncheon date or of leaving the house. I had never hit it off so quickly and so thoroughly with a woman in my entire life. Before I completely realized what was happening, I heard myself asking Tina out for dinner that night—and what was even more incredible, I heard her accepting."

When Dave finally left her home at four that afternoon to drive back to his office, his angel seemed almost to be chirping happiness: *"It is as it has been written. She is the one for whom we have waited. She is the one for whom we have saved you!"*

Dave stated in his written account of his

angelically inspired courtship with Tina that everything seemed to work out as if some heavenly screenwriter was daily turning out the pages of a cosmic script that the two mortals were following to the letter.

"We loved the same music, the same movies, the same foods, the same everything, it seemed. To use the old cliché, we truly did seem to be two peas in the same pod. I had never felt so natural, so at ease with a woman.

"And her kids— Tammy and Rodney— they were marvelous. The very notion of seeing a lady with two rug rats would normally have terrified me. But they were respectful and well-behaved— and they genuinely seemed to like me."

Dave admitted, though, that his angel's comments about his "seed" not being proper troubled him greatly.

"I'm kind of embarrassed to admit it, but I had never really read the Bible all that much. You know, a few passages here and there. And I had never been what anyone would call a literary kind of guy.

"I called a friend of mine who had once studied for the priesthood, but who had left over his honest problem with the celibacy requirement. After the usual exchange of the social amenities, I asked him to consider, theoretically, what an angel might mean if she or he referred to a person's 'seed.'

"Once I convinced my buddy that I had not been drinking and that I was really serious, and really wanted to know, he told me the answer was easy. Throughout the Bible, a man's 'seed' referred to his semen, his ability to propagate the species, to reproduce."

Dave thanked his friend, then hung up the telephone more troubled than before.

"My angel had always seemed to know everything about me. But now she was saying that there was something wrong with my semen."

Dave decided not to distress himself any further over the matter. He left a sample of his semen at a local clinic and awaited the report from his doctor.

"My angel was right as always. The lab tests came back that I was sterile, and I remembered the really severe case of mumps that I had had as a teenager. It was just as my angel had advised me: If I wanted to be a father, I would have to adopt children. So, I reasoned, what better children to adopt than the terrific kids of the woman who I was truly beginning to love with all my heart and soul!"

Dave Ragan married Tina Mattes in December of 1987. Six-year-old Tammy was a junior bridesmaid and four-year-old Rodney walked a smooth course down the aisle as the ring-bearer.

"Just before we were married, I told Tina that my guardian angel had picked her out for me years ago and had been shepherding me into her corral ever since we met.

"Tina only smiled and said, 'Then ours should truly be a marriage made in Heaven.' "

Dave said that he still receives intuitive hunches. He is convinced that they come from his guardian angel, but the last time he heard her sweet angelic voice inside his head was when Tina was coming down the aisle on the arm of her father to stand beside him at the altar.

"Well done," I heard her say. *"Well done!"*

Seven

Tender Loving Care
from Heaven

William Mandel and Eve Jacobs had known each other for several years and had become good friends long before they had begun to think of each other as potential lovers.

"When that awareness did come," Eve said, "it came suddenly, to both of us at once; and it seemed so natural that we could not help chiding ourselves for the three years of high school, four years of college, and two years working together in the same real-estate office— nine years in all— that we had wasted by not going out with each other!"

Eve remembered that William used to pronounce solemnly around the stem of his briar pipe that a Force-Greater-Than-They had seen fit for some reason to keep them apart— yet together— for nine years.

"I sometimes blushed at the memories of the many past occasions when I had taken my love-life problems to William, who, at the time, had seemed like an older brother in whom I could confide," Eve said.

When William proposed marriage, Eve did not hesitate to say yes. They would both be twenty-six in July. They had known each other for eleven years and had been dating for nearly two. They had not fallen in love; they had grown in love.

Then, two months before the wedding in August of 1973, William was killed in an automobile accident.

"I was left absolutely shattered by William's death," Eve said. "It was nearly eighteen months before I even thought of dating again.

"Two years later, after I had begun to go out somewhat steadily with Owen Laverty, he asked me to marry him. We had only been dating for about three months, and I asked for some time to consider his proposal. I felt that given time I would be able to love Owen, but I did not wish to marry him just then."

Eve explained her feelings to Owen, but the man continued to court her persistently for nearly two years. Finally, she agreed to marry her patient suitor.

Then, less than a week before the wedding . . .

"I lay tossing and turning in bed, unable to sleep," Eve said. "My mind was full of thoughts of William, my dead fiancé, rather than of Owen, my living husband-to-be.

"My entire being seemed to be permeated by a strange uneasiness. How I wished that William might be there to discuss the matter with me, to give me sage counsel as he had so often in the past. In spite of myself, I began to weep."

In between her sobbings, Eve was certain that she could hear William's voice calling her name.

"I sat bolt upright in bed, struck with the sudden realization that I was not imagining the sound of his voice. *I was actually hearing William calling to me!*"

She looked in the direction from which the voice seemed to be coming, and she was startled to see William standing solid as life next to her dresser.

"So many incredible images swirled through my brain that for a moment or two, I thought that I might succumb to the shock of seeing William standing there.

"Then I became strangely pacified at the sound of his voice.

"Your marriage to Owen is a serious mistake. You must not marry Owen Laverty. He is not the man for you. He is not the man that he appears to be."

Eve was so moved by the apparition of her dead fiancé that she feigned illness and told Owen that they must postpone their marriage in order to give her the necessary time to recuperate.

"Two weeks later, Owen was arrested on a charge of illegally possessing marijuana and of selling heroin and cocaine. During his hearing, evidence was produced that would convict him of being a drug dealer.

"As if that were not bad enough to have justified William's warning from beyond the grave," Eve added, "subsequent investigation revealed that Owen was already married and had a wife in prison. That poor woman, whose existence had been previously unknown to me, had become a drug addict under the ministrations of Owen Laverty."

Two years later, Eve said, Tom Shields asked her to marry him.

"This time I felt almost certain that an apparition of William, my guardian angel on the other side, would once again appear to advise me whether or not my choice was a wise one. I was praying that the spirit of my dear friend and lover would not manifest to inform me that Tom was some kind of secret monster.

"Three nights before our August 1978 wedding, William appeared in my room. He looked just as solid as he had when he materialized two years before. I was not shocked this time, and I waited eagerly for some sign of communication from him.

"This time William only smiled, waved a hand in farewell, and disappeared. I knew that dear William had given my marriage to Tom Shields his blessing."

Eight

Careful Attention to Her Angel

As her friends judged her according to her outer life, Doris Barnes was as normal as blueberry pie. In fact, when she was in high school, she was viewed as the all-American girl. She was an excellent student, co-captain of the varsity cheerleaders, president of the junior class; and when she was a senior, she was elected Homecoming Queen.

But Doris had a secret that she kept from even her closest friends. Ever since she was five years old, she had been in steady communication with an angel.

"I remember it all began a few nights before Christmas in 1956 when we left our comfortable little town to drive to Omaha to look at the holiday lights in the big city," Doris told me. "I looked up at the night sky and said in a wistful voice, 'I want to go home.' And then I started to cry."

Her parents and her older brother misunderstood her. They thought the five-year-old meant their cozy four-bedroom home on Baker Terrace.

"I meant the stars," Doris explained. "I suddenly had a clear image that my true home was in Heaven, somewhere beyond the stars. When I tried to tell them that I meant my home in Heaven, not my home in Nebraska, my folks got all upset, fearing that I had some premonition of my impending death. I remember that the very next day they took me to see the doctor for a complete medical checkup."

Then, on Christmas Eve, shortly after she had been tucked in bed to dream of Santa coming down the chimney with gifts, the angel materialized in her room.

"The truly weird part is that Mom was just leaving the room when the being appeared. Throughout the entire time that the angel presented itself to me, Mom stood frozen, paralyzed, right next to her. I say 'her,' because the entity appeared to me to be a female. Now that I am much older, I might say rather that the angel was basically androgynous in appearance."

Doris recalled that the angel's essential message at that time was that there was a God in Heaven who loved all little children and that she had a guardian angel who was assigned to look after her.

"The beautiful being said that there were many things that she would teach me in the years to come—and that I should never be frightened by her appearances," Doris said. "She said that I would not be able to summon her at my will, but that she would come to visit me according to some kind of heavenly plan."

As would occur to most small children to ask, Doris wanted to know what her angel's name was.

"She told me that angels didn't really have names the way little boys and girls did, but she said that I could call her Zena."

It was after that first visitation that Doris began to experience a really strong sense of her true self, her soul, belonging more to some other place.

"At that age, of course, I could only express myself by telling people that Heaven was my true home. Folks in our small Nebraska town just thought that I was a very religious little girl."

The angelic being kept her word and manifested many times to Doris.

"Sometimes Zena would just appear beside my bed at night. On other occasions, she would seem to come through the walls or the ceiling.

"When I was eleven or twelve, she began to take me with her on marvelous journeys to what I could only assume— and still do— were other worlds, other dimensions, other universes. I remember clearly one time going with her right through the glass of a closed window and wondering how she was able to accomplish such a feat."

Doris told me that on a number of occasions she was provided with physical proof of her incredible voyages with her angelic guide.

"Once I returned with an acorn in my hand after we had visited some great forest in the northwest. Another time, my angel took me to see the awesome red-rock country of Sedona, Arizona, and I came back with a small red pebble that I had picked up from a hillside."

Doris attributes her ease with her classroom lessons and her homework to the "mind expansion" that she received from her angel.

"I also received lessons in humility, graciousness, and love of all things on the planet, but about the time I was turning fifteen, I began to wonder about boys and going out on dates. Zena told me that I could be 'social,' but I should not allow myself to become serious about any of the boys in my high school. She said that there was someone special for me and I would meet him in 'the fullness of time.'"

When she was sixteen, Doris began to have vivid dreams of a young man with light brown hair who walked with a slight limp.

"He seemed very pleasant, quite good-looking; and I had many dreams about meeting him and being with him. I kind of hoped that this particular guy wasn't my dream man, because at that time I was really into physical fitness and body consciousness. I was a varsity cheerleader, cheering on all those great young athletes with their terrific bodies. I knew that I would always have an active lifestyle, and I wanted someone who would be able to keep up with me."

As she entered her late teens, the angel's visitations grew much less frequent.

"I can remember seeing her only twice during my senior year of high school. I don't think I saw Zena at all during my first year in college. My sophomore year, I saw her just once.

"Although I was still certain that I 'felt' her presence and was aware of her guidance on some level of consciousness, I was kind of concerned. I knew very well that I had not outgrown my need for angelic counsel, but I also remembered Zena saying that I must never become too dependent upon her. A very important lesson in our education on Earth was to learn to be self-reliant and resourceful."

At the beginning of her junior year, Doris told me that she began for the first time to read the Bible regularly. I was quite surprised to hear this, as I assumed that the angel had taken pains to see to her religious education.

"No, Brad," Doris answered my query. "Zena saw to my *spiritual* education. She spoke always along very universal lines, never advocating the path of any particular earthly religious expression. She emphasized ethics, morality, and unconditional love.

"To love another person unconditionally is probably the hardest thing for us humans to practice. For us, love is almost always conditional. You know, 'I'll love you— if you love me back.' Even as parents we too often permit our children to infer that we love them only when they are behaving in the manner that we wish them to act."

Although the angel's appearances were less frequent, Doris said that the dreams of the handsome young man with the light brown hair had increased.

"Sometimes it almost seemed as if I were living two lives in two different dimensions. The one was the rather dull academic routine of a college student. The other was a much more romantic existence as an explorer of some sort, traveling over mountain trails, hacking through jungle growth, digging through ancient ruins— all in the company of this man my angel had said was my prearranged mate."

Since I knew her as Doris Barnes Zemke, I knew that we had to be coming to the part of her story where she met Gary and lived happily ever after.

"Not so fast, Brad," she laughed. "If only life were that easy. If only I had listened to my guardian angel."

Doris explained that toward the end of her senior year in college she had begun to go steady with a bright and attractive business major from Kankakee, Illinois.

"Ted seemed to be the right man for me. He had light brown hair, was co-captain of the men's tennis team, and he didn't have a limp. I figured that my dream lover's limp must have been symbolic of some other lesson that Zena had been trying to teach me as a fifteen-year-old, and I rationalized—against the argument of that 'still, small voice' within me—that Ted was the man that the angels had destined for me."

Doris confessed to me that Zena had manifested physically before her for the first time in two years, shortly before her wedding to Ted.

"Zena told me that I had not chosen well, but since I had chosen, I must receive the lessons of that relationship for my good and my gaining. When I argued that Ted had *seemed* to be the man that she had shown me in my dreams, Zena just gave me this cold look, like you might give a petulent child that won't listen.

"I knew that it wasn't too late to call off the wedding, but I just really felt stubborn. Like, what did an angel know about love and marriage and sex and babies anyway?"

To Doris's dismay, it turned out that her angel guide was better informed about such matters after several thousand years of experience than she was at the pseudo-sophisticated age of twenty-three.

"The first couple of years were not too bad. Ted was on the road a lot, but I found out that even then he had begun seeing other women in various cities. Although he made me fairly comfortable in the material sense—and he made two beautiful babies with me—

he made my life a hell on the spiritual and psychological levels.

"After a few years, Ted came down with a very serious social disease due to his infidelities. Thank God that was before AIDS was rampant— and thank God he hadn't transmitted the illness to me. I divorced him in 1979."

In 1981, Doris and her two daughters moved to the San Francisco area. She was able to secure a good job in a bookstore, and one night she was asked by a friend to attend a lecture by Gary Zemke, who had just returned from spending two years in the Brazilian rain forests with the native people of the region.

"I was very moved by the fire and passion in this man's voice as he showed us slides of the wholesale destruction of a vital natural resource— destruction that was already beginning to blight the rain forests," Doris told me. "Afterward as luck would have it, I was among seven or eight people who accompanied him for coffee after his presentation. As we were walking to the restaurant, I could not help noticing that he walked with a slight limp."

It was then for the first time that Doris actually saw how much more accurately Gary Zemke fit the description of the soulmate that her angel guide Zena had projected in her dreams.

"Later, much later, the others had left the restaurant one by one; and it was only Gary and me alone in the booth, sipping our umpteenth cup of coffee.

"He had begun to tell me of what he considered to be his larger spiritual mission— to visit what he believed to be the most sacred power places of the world. He told me that he had felt certain ever since his earliest childhood that he was to discover some artifact of the magnitude of the Lost Ark of the Covenant that would serve to convince millions of the reality of the partnership between the worlds of the physical and the nonphysical. Until that most momentous occasion, he had decided to establish a tour business that would take spiritual seekers on odysseys of awareness to various sacred locations."

As the night drew on to a beautiful close, Gary confessed to Doris that he had been drawn to her from the moment that he had seen her enter the lecture hall. He kissed her gently before he put her in a cab, and they had agreed to meet again the next night.

"It was not, I believe, until our fourth or fifth time together, that I very discreetly asked Gary what accident or circumstances had given him the limp.

"He smiled and said that he hoped that I

would not think him a nut, but he would tell me the whole story."

In brief, Gary had been hiking a narrow trail in the Andes Mountains of Peru when he had lost his footing and fell.

"It was a long drop to the next outcropping," he told Doris. "I would have been killed—surely received more than a leg broken in three places—if my fall had not been broken in a most wonderful manner."

"Yes, yes," Doris prompted him. "Go on."

"Do you believe in miracles?"

Doris assured Gary that she did.

"Well," he went on cautiously, "I actually saw my guardian angel materialize and break my fall. If it had not been for those angelic wings cushioning my body, I am certain that I would surely have been killed on those rocks."

Gary laughed nervously, never taking his eyes from Doris's face. "Can you believe an angel? I mean, that an angel, my guardian angel, actually materialized and saved my life in the Andes Mountains?"

Doris smiled at the memory. "Well, Brad," she said, concluding her story, "I reached out for Gary's hand and told him that I had absolutely no problem believing in angels manifesting to assist us in our time of trouble. I kissed him, and then asked him if he believed that angels could also serve as match-makers?"

Doris and Gary Zemke have been married now for eleven years, fully cognizant that they were brought together to share their lives as one by the beautiful ministry of the Angels of Love.

Nine

Street Angel's Mission

When Edward Neumann was five years old and playing in the backyard of his childhood home in Hartford, Connecticut, he saw a figure that he first supposed was Jesus.

"The being seemed to be standing on a small white cloud," he told me. "The cloud was suspended about five or six feet in the air, and the figure held out his arms in a kind of 'come unto me' type of gesture."

Edward remembered vividly that the entity was dressed in a white robe with a purple sash that came down across his right shoulder to drape about his waist.

"Although the being had long reddish-brown hair, he had no beard; and all the pictures that I had seen of Jesus depicted him with a beard," Edward said. "That's when I decided that the entity was not Jesus, but an angel."

Edward experienced similar visitations on six different occasions during his childhood.

"I was not conscious of any words spoken by the entity during these early visits, but I was always left feeling that I had been born to fulfill some kind of special purpose on Earth."

When Edward was twelve, the family's dog, a feisty little rat terrier named Muggs, was struck by an automobile and dealt a severe injury.

"I cried my eyes out when I found little Muggs in the backyard. He had dragged himself home and was whimpering softly. Blood trickled from between his clamped jaws, and I knew that he was dying."

When his mother came home from work and found Edward out back with the badly injured Muggs, she openly shared her son's grief; but she said that they would have to take the dog to the veterinarian's to be put to sleep just as soon as his father got home. Edward fell to his knees and began to pray for Muggs's recovery.

"I begged God over and over to let Muggs be okay again. The little dog was my constant companion, and I could not bear to think of coming home from school night after night and not finding Muggs there to greet me."

Edward remembered clearly that after nearly two hours of continuous prayer, the angelic being appeared before him.

"His mouth did not move, but I heard *inside* my head his words of instruction. He told me to put my hands on Muggs and to send thoughts of healing into his body while I prayed for his recovery."

The boy was astonished to see Muggs suddenly stand up on all fours and walk toward his food dish as if nothing had happened to him.

"Inside my head, I heard the angel tell me that part of my mission on Earth was to serve as a healer. I thanked God over and over for allowing Muggs to come back to life. Later, when Dad got home, he tried to tell me that such things often happened to dogs. They might be hit by a car, badly stunned for a while, then bounce back to consciousness and be none the worse for wear. I knew better, though. I could even see that Muggs had a kind of glow around him for the next three or four days."

Edward told his younger brother Dick how the angel had helped him heal Muggs.

"Dick was only seven, but he was still pretty much of a realist. He doubted me at first, but I told him that I could get rid of his stomachache. When he was that age, it seemed as though he was always suffering from upset stomachs and digestive problems, so I put my hand on his tummy and prayed for five or six minutes. 'Hey, man,' Dick grinned. 'It works!' From that moment on, I became Dick's official healer—and as word spread among the kids, the medicine man for most of the neighborhood."

About five or six weeks after Edward had revealed his gift of healing, the Neumann family received word of the death of Uncle Karl in Los Angeles.

"Uncle Karl was Dad's younger brother, and Dick and I just loved him. We were really torn up by the news of his death. Mom and Dad were going to fly out for the funeral, but because of the prohibitive cost, Dick and I were to stay with a neighbor lady, a widow who sometimes looked after us when our folks were out of town.

"The night after we had got word of Uncle Karl's death, we lay upstairs in our beds feeling really sad. Dick started crying and saying how he wished that we could have seen Karl just one last time. 'If only we could have been able to say good-bye and to tell him how much we loved him,' Dick kept saying over and over."

Edward began to pray with all the intensity that he had mentally exerted to heal Muggs.

"I asked my angel if we just couldn't see Uncle Karl's soul before it went to Heaven. I prayed and prayed with all my might, begging for the chance to be able to say good-bye to our beloved uncle."

After about an hour of such intense prayers, the boys began to notice a glowing ball about two feet in diameter beginning to form in a corner of their room. Within two to three minutes, they were able to distinguish very clearly the images of Edward's angelic guide and their uncle Karl.

"At first Dick hid under the covers, but I told him not to be afraid, that God had granted our wish and sent my angel to escort Uncle Karl to see us one last time. Uncle Karl smiled and waved good-bye. We told him that we loved him, and we could read his lips when he said that he loved us, too. And then the angel, the glowing ball, and Uncle Karl just disappeared.

"You know, I'm now thirty-eight years old and Dick is thirty-one; but not too long ago when he was here for a visit, he talked about that materialization of the angel and Uncle Karl and told me that whenever his faith in God or the afterlife began to waver, he just remembered that incredible manifestation and everything is all right in his personal universe."

* * *

Edward continued to receive occasional tutorial sessions with his angel guide throughout his adolescent years.

"My angel counseled me to conduct my work rather quietly while I was in high school. I would stop nosebleeds, heal kids' bumps and bruises, banish headaches and upset stomachs— low-key stuff like that."

When I met Edward in 1986, he was a full-time massage therapist, widely known as the man with a remarkable healing touch, "Mister Magic Hands."

"I knew that I must be of service to others, and this seemed to me like the best way to be able to heal subtly and quietly, just like my angel directed me. Sometimes a client will come to me for a massage, 'just to relax,' to 'remove stress.' But I'll pick up on something going wrong in his body that is really serious. After a couple sessions, my angel gives me a 'green light,' and I know that we have taken care of the more complicated problem."

In 1988, when Edward first placed his "magic" fingers on Margarete Jackson, he experienced a series of internal shocks.

"It was like tiny electrical shocks that zinged me whenever I touched her. I *knew* that this lady was someone really special— and someone who was going to be very important in my life."

* * *

Now happily married to Edward for four years, Margarete told me that she had been employed as a bank teller at the time that she met him.

"The new manager was a real jerk. He would hit on me for dates, then when I refused, he would find something in my work to complain about.

"On this particular day, I had stormed out of the bank on my lunch hour angry as a wet cat. The pompous toad had just humiliated me in front of several customers and my fellow employees on some minute and meaningless technicality. I didn't know if I should hand in my resignation, file a formal complaint, or grin and bear it. I really didn't know what I was going to do."

She bought a hot dog from a street vendor, took two bites, and tossed it in a garbage can. On top of everything else, it was beginning to rain.

Margarete remembered that a nondescript street hustler approached her with a handbill. "Check it out! It'll make you feel good. Cure what ails you," he told her as he thrust a sheet of blue paper in her hands.

She crumpled the sheet in her hand, assuming it to be an advertisement for some sordid sex show or a closing-out sale for a merchant who had been going out of business regularly for the past seventeen years.

"No, ma'am," the hustler admonished her quietly. "You really should read that sheet of paper."

Startled by his quiet authority, Margarete smoothed out the handbill and saw that it advertised the services of a massage therapist named Edward Neumann and extolled the virtues of his techniques for relieving stress and tension.

"At first the handbill intrigued me," she said. "Lord knows I needed something to relieve stress and tension— before I walked back into the bank and clobbered the jerk with the right hook that my father had taught me when I was sixteen. But could I trust someone who advertised in the streets? I mean, I had heard all about massage parlor scams for men. Perhaps this Neumann guy had come up on a variation to please frustrated women."

And then Margarete glanced up and saw that she now found herself on the street where, according to the handbill, Neumann's office was located. In fact, she was only two or three doors down from it.

An elderly woman stood outside the door of his office, stretching her arms above her head and smiling broadly.

"Oh, dearie," she said to Margarete, "that was wonderful. What a marvelous session.

That Mr. Neumann is just remarkable, just plain remarkable. I feel like a new woman—and that's a fact."

Margarete paused to read the handbill again, slowly, more deliberately. It certainly seemed as though this Neumann fellow had what she needed right now. And the elderly woman didn't seem as though she would tolerate any hanky-panky.

When she looked up to ask the woman a few questions, she was surprised to see that the lady was nowhere in sight.

"I figured that she must have grabbed a cab while I was busy reading the handbill," Margarete said, "so I thought, What the heck! and decided to go inside."

Edward perceived at once that the electrical shocks that he was picking up from his new client were his angel's way of telling him that this was the special woman who had been sent to him by the Angels to enrich his life.

"And you know what, Brad?" Margarete asked me rhetorically. "We had been dating regularly for months before I found out that Edward *had never* printed any handbills to advertise his massage therapy. He said that he had always assumed—as I had done—that people would misinterpret the true nature of his services if he had utilized such a method of advertising."

Edward nodded, adding that he had relied solely on word of mouth to bring him more than enough clients to keep him extremely busy. "I had only advertised once or twice in some alternate city newspapers— and I was flooded by the response. I absolutely never would have employed street hawkers to push my business."

But both Margarete and Edward agreed that it was quite apparent that his angel had no such compunctions if such an action would serve the angelic purpose of bringing them together.

Ten

Just in Time

"Tim Martindale literally swept me off my feet," Phyllis Schneider confessed in her account of her strange experience with an angelic guide. "I was not yet twenty and very inexperienced in the ways of love. Tim was nearly nine years older than I, and he seemed to be the very epitome of masculine charm and strength."

Phyllis was even more pleased when her parents also warmed to her beau.

"Tim told Dad that he was an avid fisherman—a passion that was shared by our entire family—and soon he had become a part of our family outings at the lake."

By midsummer, Tim and Phyllis were at

the "engaged-to-be-engaged" state of their courtship.

Phyllis had met Tim at a dance that had been held at a nearby resort. Since Tim lived in a city that was quite some distance from Phyllis, he had to drive a good number of miles to see her. Because of the problem of the miles that separated them, they seldom saw each other during the week.

"But after Tim had so ingratiated himself to my parents, he began to stay the weekends with us," Phyllis said.

One Thursday night before he was coming to stay with the Schneiders, Tim called to ask Phyllis if her parents would mind keeping a trunk of his personal possessions in their attic storeroom.

"That way," he explained, "I'll always have shirts and ties and a toothbrush available— and I won't have to be hauling so much stuff back and forth with me."

Such a request made good sense to the Schneiders, and permission was readily granted.

"By late summer, though, I was beginning to have vague feelings of discomfort in regard to my charming and persistent suitor," Phyllis explained.

One night as the couple parked beside the lake, she was becoming annoyed with Tim's insistence on making love.

His hands had been roaming her body with gentle insistence, his fingers gently probing and touching sensitive areas. The combination of his mouth on her own and the steady, sensual pressure of his fingers had kindled a fire within her that Phyllis knew could only be extinguished by the act of physical love.

"As old-fashioned as it might have seemed to others of my generation," she said, "I had always vowed that I would wait until I had a wedding band around my finger before I allowed any man to claim my virginity. But Tim had already unbuttoned my blouse, and the fingers of one of his hands were tugging at the hook of my bra while the fingers of the other were at the zipper of my slacks."

That was when Phyllis called a halt to the proceedings. Tim seemed just too damned experienced.

"Tim," she asked him bluntly, "have you had a lot of women before me?"

His only answer was a kind of chuckle deep in his throat that seemed to Phyllis to sound too prideful.

"Well," she persisted, "have you ever been married before?"

Tim's hands became suddenly inactive. He leaned back against the seat with a sigh of resignation. "Why do you keep asking me that? I've told you the answer to that question a hundred times. N-O. No. I have never been married. Don't you believe me?"

Phyllis shrugged away his objections. "You are nearly twenty-nine. People do get married, you know."

She could see his perfect teeth in the dim illumination from the dashboard. Tim was smiling at her. Such wonderfully white teeth, she sighed mentally. Such a handsome, tanned face. Such a great guy.

"Of course people get married," Tim teased. "That's why I want to marry you."

There was something in his voice just then. Just a slight tonal disharmony . . . just a minor variation in frequency that caused her to ask the question one more time.

"But have *you* ever been married before?"

Tim did not answer until he had shaken a cigarette from a hard pack in his coat pocket and placed it between his lips.

"Okay," he said. "I was married once before."

He touched the glowing coils of the lighter to the cigarette, exhaled a cloud of smoke.

Phyllis thought that her heart had stopped beating. "His words had been like a sword that pierced through my chest and cut my heart in two. But it started beating again with his next words."

"I was married to a pretty young blond girl . . . who died in childbirth."

"Oh, Tim," Phyllis said sincerely. "I'm sorry."

She felt at once ashamed that she had finally wrung the truth from him—and disappointed that he had not told her before about his previous marriage.

"And . . . the child?"

"Peter," he answered, expelling the name in another cloud of cigarette smoke. "He lives with my mother. He's six years old."

Phyllis swallowed hard. If they married after her birthday in December, she would be a twenty-year-old bride with a six-year-old stepson.

Oh, well. He was Tim's son, and she loved Tim.

"Peter must come live with us just as soon as we're married," she blurted out.

Tim grabbed her happily, gave her a long kiss. "Name the date," he said. "Just name the date. And Peter can come and live with us . . . right *after* our honeymoon!"

The night that she decided on December sixteenth as their wedding date, Phyllis said that she had "the most terrible kind of nightmare."

"I dreamed that I had married Tim and we had gone away to live in our own home. Then Tim began to build a cage around me, and I began to scream hysterically. But whenever I would scream too loudly, a group of nurses would appear from nowhere and tell me to be quiet or they would stick me with their long needles. And all the while Tim kept building the cage around me—until, at last, I saw that it was not a cage at all. It was a coffin!"

Even after she awakened, Phyllis knew that she was not alone in her room.

"I nearly screamed when I saw a strange figure outlined with a silver light standing at the foot of my bed," Phyllis said. "I could distinguish no features—and when I sat up to turn on the bedlamp, the ghostly thing had vanished."

The next night turned out to be a carbon copy of the previous one.

"First, I had the strange, jumbled, frightening nightmare, then I awakened to find the eerily glowing figure at the foot of my bed. I began to fear that I might be losing my mind."

On the third night, Phyllis stated in her account of the experience, the same nightmare seized her. Tim set about building the cage that surrounded her . . . the nurses appeared to threaten her with their long needles . . . and she discovered the cage was really a coffin.

"It was at that point each night that I

would awaken," she said. "And on the third night, I heard a voice calling to me. The shimmering image stood before me— only this time I could make out long, reddish brown hair flowing down to the broad shoulders of an angel, a being of light that was very commanding in appearance."

In an authoritative voice, the angel told her that she must not marry Tim.

"You will only *think* that you will be his wife, but you will be wrong."

Phyllis asked the angel what he meant by such a statement.

"He still has another wife. She is not dead. She is *not* dead."

And then suddenly there appeared with the angel the image of a tall, pretty young woman with long blond hair. Although she was dressed in some kind of shapeless gown, it was evident that she had a good figure.

It was her eyes that most disturbed Phyllis. They looked dazed, confused— almost as if she were some kind of hunted animal.

And then both the angel and the pretty young blond woman disappeared.

Sleep for Phyllis the rest of the night was an impossibility. She sat up in bed, staring until dawn at the space where the illuminated being had stood and issued its dire warning— and where the blond woman had materialized and disappeared so suddenly.

That morning over breakfast she told her mother and her fifteen-year-old sister Becky about her terrible nocturnal experiences of the past three nights. Because they had always been a religious family, Phyllis had no reluctance in describing in detail the somber warning that she had received from an angelic being.

"Look in his trunk in the attic," declared Becky, who read far too many gothic romances. "I'll bet you'll find a key to Tim's terrible secret in that trunk."

Phyllis was surprised when her mother agreed with Becky.

"I know it seems like a violation of the ethics which Dad and I have tried to instill in you girls," her mother said, "but it just may be that there might be some kind of clue to Tim's past in that trunk."

Her mother did insist that they wait until their father returned from work to investigate the contents of the trunk, however.

"When I told Dad about the appearance of the angel and the young woman and the angelic being's warning not to marry Tim, he quickly agreed with the consensus to open the trunk in the attic.

"We knew that Tim kept the key to the trunk with him, but Dad had an old friend who was an accomplished locksmith and who could be trusted to be discreet," Phyllis said.

"In one compartment of the trunk, we found an insurance policy that was still in force for a Mrs. Cindy Martindale. There was another policy on Tim which named Mrs. Martindale as the beneficiary. We all knew that no one pays premiums on policies on a deceased wife— nor does one declare a dead woman a beneficiary.

"Then Mother found a number of receipts which had been paid to a sanatorium in a nearby state. It all became very clear that Tim's wife had not died in childbirth. Rather, she had suffered a nervous breakdown after the birth of their son."

Although she feared that it would be like turning a knife in her flesh, Phyllis asked her parents to accompany her to the sanatorium so that she might verify the circumstantial evidence with firsthand investigation.

"Mom and Dad consented, and we set out on the long drive to the mental hospital.

"Dad used the pretext that we were old family friends, and we were given permission to visit Tim's wife, Cindy."

Phyllis was shocked when they entered the hospital room to find the same tall, pretty blond woman whose image that the angel had materialized in her bedroom.

"Thank God, we had somehow managed to choose a day when she was enjoying a period relatively free from trauma and delusion."

Phyllis and her parents chatted with Cindy about her husband and her son, and Phyllis was grateful that her parents had come along to bear the burden of the conversation.

"Dad told the woman that Tim had been very busy and had been working long hours, but that he sent his love.

"I could not hold back the tears when Cindy smiled and nodded. Then said very quietly, 'Tell Tim that I love him, too. But he hasn't been to see me for so long. Please . . . please tell him to come to see me. He . . . he acts like I'm dead.' "

Phyllis concluded her account by stating that her father called Tim that very night when they returned to their home.

"Dad told him to come to pick up his trunk and not to try to see me ever again. I heard Dad urge Tim to take a greater interest in the wife and son whom he was shamefully neglecting.

"Later, Dad told me that Tim had become furious with us for 'meddling in his private life,' and he had demanded who had told us of his wife in the institution. Tim knew very well that we had no common friends, and no one among his friends knew that he had been seeing me.

"Dad simply told him that an 'interested

party' who had wanted to keep me from misery and shame had decided to intervene.

"I felt that Dad's way of describing the visitation of the angel in my bedroom was as good as any."

Eleven

The Greatest Gift

Judith Richardson Haimes, one of the nation's leading psychic-sensitives, told me this touching story of how the Angels of Love granted Kathy Palmer's and Mike Alexander's wish for a perfect love— if only for a little while on Earth.

Kathy Palmer was a pretty girl of twenty-seven with large, dark blue eyes and a slim, but shapely, figure. She was certainly not a young woman who would blend into a crowd, but because she was so painfully shy she did not have a very interesting social life.

She caught an awful "bug" that had been going around, and it had left her weak, tired, and a little depressed. On this particular day, she was feeling very low in energy, and because her car was being repaired, she had to take the bus to work.

The job she had as a "Girl Friday" for a medical supply company did not challenge her intellectually, but it was not at all unpleasant, and the hours and the pay were good.

As she was riding the bus to work, the tall young man sitting on the aisle seat beside her seemed to be trying very hard to make conversation. As lonely as she had been recently, Kathy was still not so desperate that she would succumb to a flirtation on the bus—even if he was distinctly handsome and very well dressed.

Her attention was directed to a number of young couples who were holding hands as they walked along the street. Some couples were pushing baby carriages. They all seemed so very much in love, and Kathy felt a twinge of envy.

"Now this is something. Isn't this terrific? I love these kinds of stories," the handsome man sitting next to her was saying as he pointed a forefinger at some news item in the morning paper.

Curious, Kathy smiled and inquired about what newspaper article had so pleased him.

"Here is a family who recently became homeless," he said, his voice mounting in enthusiasm, "and then *bingo!* Overnight, they became millionaires."

"Did they win the lottery?" Kathy wondered, laughing at her anonymous companion's vicarious excitement over a desperate family's good fortune.

"You're absolutely right!" he told her, grinning at her as if she were a genius with remarkable insight. "They won the six-million-dollar lottery."

The stranger folded the newspaper on his lap. "My name is Ian, by the way."

She almost shocked herself by engaging in even a brief conversation with a total stranger. "I'm Kathy."

"You know," the man was rambling on, "if I could have just one wish, I would wish to win the lottery."

Kathy shook her head. "Money can't make everyone happy."

"Oh, really!" Ian laughed. "And what would you wish for, Kathy? What would be your one wish?"

As the bus slowed in heavy traffic, Kathy pointed out the window at a couple holding hands and looking into one another's eyes as if they were the only two people on the planet.

"See that man and woman standing there in front of the jewelry store? That's what I want. That would be my wish. If I could have just one wish, I would ask for someone to love me like that and . . ."

Startled by her frank admission to a stranger and quite embarrassed by her forwardness, Kathy was relieved to see that the bus had reached her stop.

"This is my stop," she said as she stepped over Ian's long legs. "I must get off here."

She walked up to the door as the bus pulled to a halt. Kathy glanced back at the row of seats that she had just vacated and sought out the handsome stranger to whom she had uttered her bold confession.

His seat was empty.

Her eyes moved quickly about the bus, moving past the remaining passengers.

Ian was nowhere to be seen.

Puzzled, Kathy stepped from the bus. She hurried into her building, wondering if perhaps she might have dozed off for a moment and dreamed the entire embarrassing conversation with the stranger. After all, her bout with the illness had left her somewhat listless and low in energy. Maybe she had just dreamed about a bold conversation with a handsome stranger.

* * *

When he left for work that day, Mike Alexander felt as if his heart would break. He had never wanted to hurt Abby. After all, he had *a* love for her— even though he was certain that he was not *in* love with her.

Abby and Mike had grown up across the street from each other. They had gone to the same schools; they had all of the same friends; and they even shared the same profession. They were both accountants and they were employed by the same firm.

For years they had been pals, buddies, friends. But for the past year, Mike had found thoughts of another woman strongly subverting the fondness that he felt for Abby.

Perhaps he was foolish. He only saw this woman once a week when he visited the medical supply company in which she worked. Her boss, Karl Fine, was one of his regular clients; and the first time that he set his eyes on Kathy Palmer, Fine's Girl Friday, her image was freeze-framed into his brain.

Although he had never even asked Kathy for a date, he was attracted to her in a way that made his heart race just thinking about her. He knew that he could never have such feelings for Abby.

So last night, when he and Abby talked for six hours and shared their true feelings with one another, he learned that she, too, wanted to separate. She, too, had noticed that they made much better friends than lovers.

As Mike drove to work, he felt a little topsy-turvy with his emotions, but, thank God, it was Friday. The bright spot in his day would be seeing Kathy, the light of his heart— even though she had no idea how he felt.

And when the temporary at the medical supply company told him that Kathy had left early to go to the doctor, he spiraled into a dismal funk.

Feeling too depressed to go straight home after work, Mike headed for a place where he could get an order of chicken wings and a couple of beers.

A tall, dark young man came up to his table. "Hello, my name is Ian. I'll be taking your order tonight."

Before Mike could place his order for wings and beer, the talkative waiter said, "It sure was amazing about that homeless family winning the six-million-dollar lottery, wasn't it?"

Mike shrugged. "I didn't hear anything about it."

"Oh, sure," Ian said excitedly. "It was in all the papers, and it's been on the news all day. Well, I'm glad that if someone besides me had to win it was a family in such need. But boy, do I wish that I could win the lottery. If I had only one wish, that's what I would wish. I would wish to win the lottery."

Mike had to smile at the rapid-talking young waiter. "I'd like an order of wings and a beer, please."

"What would you wish for if you had only one wish?" Ian asked.

"You mean besides my chicken wings and beer?"

"I'll get those for you right away, sir. But, please, tell me what you would wish for if you had only one wish? Would you wish to win the lottery?"

Mike looked for a silent moment at the earnest young man standing before him. "Well, Ian, I guess I would wish for the woman of my dreams. And then for my beer and wings."

Ian thanked him for the order and hurried off to get the wings and beer.

Five minutes passed.

No beer. No chicken wings. No Ian.

A few minutes later, a pretty girl in a black and white uniform that looked like a cross between a scullery maid's outfit and a sailor suit came to Mike's table.

"I'm sorry, sir. We're really busy. I'm really sorry I took so long. My name is Kim, and I'll . . ."

"It's okay, Kim," Mike interrupted her spiel. "Ian has already taken my order."

"Ian?"

"Ian the waiter," Mike said a bit impatiently. "Although I think he has gone to the farm to get those chicken wings."

"We don't have a waiter named Ian working here, sir," Kim told him in a perfunctory manner. "This has been my table for the last two and a half hours now. May I take your order, please?"

Now that Abby had released Mike from any emotional obligation which he might have felt, he tossed all reluctance to the winds and called Kathy on Monday for a dinner date. He could hardly believe it when she accepted without hesitation.

Monday night's dinner date mushroomed into a dinner shared every evening for the next five days.

Kathy could not believe what a difference a week could make. It had only been that last Friday on the bus when she had told the talkative stranger her wish for true love. And now, dear God, it truly seemed as though her wish had been granted.

* * *

In less than three months, Mike and Kathy knew that they were meant to be together.

While walking on the beach at dusk one night, Mike asked her to marry him. "I want to spend the rest of my life with you."

Half-laughing, half-crying with tears of joy, Kathy answered that she accepted his proposal.

"This is my wish come true!" Mike shouted to the first stars of the evening as he took Kathy in his arms.

Over Mike's shoulder, Kathy saw a tall, handsome young man smiling at them as he passed them on the beach. There was something about him that was strangely familiar.

One year later, while sitting in Dr. Evans's office, Mrs. Kathy Alexander was filled with conflict. Both she and Mike wanted a family, but they had planned to wait a bit longer until they were a little more secure financially. But the thrill of having a baby— even unplanned— was as exciting as all the happiest moments of her life put together.

But then Dr. Evans told her that she was not pregnant.

How could that be, Kathy wanted to know. She had missed her last two cycles. She was tired all the time. She was nauseated most of the day.

Kathy felt a sense of foreboding when Dr. Evans suggested more tests.

A few days later, Mike was with her, holding her hand, when Dr. Evans told them that Kathy had very advanced ovarian cancer.

"How soon can we start treatments?" Kathy asked, trying to take control of the situation.

Dr. Evans's words seemed to ring out as if he were speaking from an echo chamber: "I am so very sorry, but my best advice to you is to accept the fact that treatment at this point would at best give you only a few weeks more . . . and they would not be very pleasant weeks. The truth of the matter is that the treatment might take up what precious little time that you have."

"How long *do* I have?" Kathy wanted to know, still trying to maintain some degree of control.

Dr. Evans said that no one could accurately predict the future, but in such advanced cases as Kathy's, one could allow six weeks to as long as three months.

After Kathy and Mike had obtained three additional "second opinions," they were ready at last to accept the inevitable.

* * *

Both Kathy and Mike were very spiritual, but neither strictly followed any religious doctrine. She was a Catholic who had not been to church in many years. She and the Church disagreed on too many points.

Mike had been brought up in a non-religious Jewish family. They were a loving and good family, albeit unceremoniously Jewish.

Kathy and Mike believed that they were soulmates who had been blessed to have found the opportunity to become complete in the short time together in their present life experience. Since they both accepted the concept of reincarnation, Kathy and Mike reconciled themselves with the thought that they would be together again in another time.

Kathy, who wanted to die at home with her beloved Mike near, was kept comfortable. The medical supply company for which Kathy had worked had an insurance plan that provided excellent home nursing care.

Kathy's mother, Nancy Palmer, brushed a wisp of hair off her sleeping daughter's forehead as she prayed the rosary. She had let the nurse's aide go early to pick up her son at school. Nurse Brown, the R.N., was due soon.

When the doorbell rang, Nancy was surprised to see a tall, handsome young man standing there. He introduced himself as Ian Baker, a nurse's aide, who had been sent to help until Nurse Brown arrived. She had been unavoidably detained.

Together they saw that Kathy was resting comfortably. While Ian checked her pulse and started to read her chart, Nancy went to the kitchen to fix herself a small lunch. It had been hours since she had eaten, and she was beginning to get a slight headache.

Mike's entire office staff said that they would pitch in and help carry his load until he returned from his extended leave of absence to be at Kathy's side. Abby had promised him that she would personally keep close tabs on all of his most important clients.

As he drove home, he reflected upon just how much his life had changed in the past year.

As he went by the restaurant where he had once stopped for chicken wings and a beer, he remembered the tall, talkative young waiter who had got him to express his wish for the love of his life.

"I got my wish," Mike said aloud, tears stinging his eyes. "If only for too short a time."

Just at that moment, a familiar face stood

out among the crowded sidewalk near the corner.

It was he— Ian or whatever his name was. The mysterious waiter who had disappeared after taking his order. There he was, a smiling face in a crowd of strangers.

The tall, dark young man waved to Mike in a familiar greeting.

Mike suddenly felt a surge of calmness and tranquility unlike anything that he had ever experienced.

There was a noise.

A flash of light.

And then it was over.

The old man never even saw Mike's car in front of him. The seventy-seven-year-old man pulled into the intersection against the light.

Someone called for an ambulance, but it was too late.

Mike Alexander was dead.

It was 3:31 P.M.

When she walked back into her daughter's room from the kitchen, Nancy Palmer at first thought something was on fire, for the room was filled with a foglike smoke.

As her eyes darted around the bedroom, she was startled to see an image of her son-in-law, Mike Alexander, standing at the bedside reaching out for Kathy.

Then a most extraordinary thing happened: Kathy sat up in bed, reached out to Mike— and at the same instant, the "mist" that just a moment before had filled the room suddenly vanished, as if sucked out by an invisible vacuum cleaner.

Still frozen in the moment, Nancy saw Kathy's bright blue eyes half-open and glazed, her lower jaw hanging open, relaxed in death.

Nancy heard a distant ringing sound.

Her eyes met those of Ian, the nurse's aide, and then she heard an awful cry like that of a wounded animal.

It was not until the gentle hand of Nurse Brown touched her shoulder that Nancy realized that the terrible cry had been coming from her own throat.

"I rang the bell," Nurse Brown explained, "but there was no answer. Kathy is gone. I am so sorry.

"I would have been here on time, but there was a very bad accident, and traffic was held up. An elderly man struck another car after running a red light."

"Where is the aide?" Nancy asked. "Where is Ian?"

"Ian?"

"The nurse's aide. He was just here a moment ago. He was standing right beside Kathy's bed."

When they first met in Brazil, Joshua did not know any Portuguese nor did Vera know any English. But through divine intervention, the two lovers discovered their destiny with each other.

Jon Marc and Anastasia Hammer found each other through the powerful spirit of love, guided by their Angel of Love, Jeshua.

As a five year-old boy, Brad Steiger experienced a powerful vision of his soulmate, Sherry Hansen. Years later, an angel posing as a "mutual friend" led Brad to her. They were married during the Harmonic Convergence in Sedona, Arizona in 1987.

Brad Steiger, author and lecturer, and Sherry Hansen Steiger, former model, author and ordained Baptist Minister, travel to the world's sacred sites on their shared journey of the spirit.

In this remarkable series of photographs, Sherry Hansen Steiger draws down the Light while she meditates on a ledge overlooking one of the vortexes in Sedona, Arizona until she becomes one with its power.

Receptive to angelic messages since she was a small child, Lori Jean never doubted the guidance that led her to her marriage with Charles Flory in July, 1985.

Lori Jean and Charles Flory with their beloved psychic animal family. From left to right: Brandy, Laddie, Stormy and Whiskers.

Captured on film with the help of her heavenly guide,
Lori Jean Flory has recorded a wonderful manifestation
of angelic energy.

Internationally famous healers, Lorraine and Victor Darr
on their honeymoon in 1950. Almost from the instant
they met, they knew they were fated for one another.

Victor and Lorraine
Darr made no
secret of their
dependence on the
Angels of Love. This
photograph was
taken in 1982.

An amazing record of angelic intervention, this photo of Victor and Lorraine Darr was taken from the inside of an apartment in a suburb of Chicago (see photo with child). However, instead of the view of city rooftops, we see a primeval forest and the loving eyes of an angel co-mingled with the image of the Darrs. Lorraine reports that she felt the presence of an angelic lightbeing named Mark around her when this picture was taken.

John Harricharan met Mardai, his wife-to-be, when she was six and he was thirteen. Separated by thousands of miles, they met again years later and fulfilled their destiny by marrying and adopting their daughter Malika and son Jonathan.

Judith Richardson Haimes, one of the nation's foremost psychic-sensitives, and her husband Dr. Allen Nelson Haimes freely admit to the divine support they have received through the years. Judith shared the account in which a handsome angel guide brought two lovers together to share their perfect love in heaven.

Fay Marvin Clark first recognized his soulmate Marvel in 1963, when she was thirty-one and he was fifty-six. However, they listened to their angels and lived their lives separately, patiently waiting until 1980 when they were finally joined in matrimony. They enjoyed eleven wonderful years before Fay was called home to heaven in 1991.

RA-Ja Dove, left and his love, Moi-RA on their wedding day in 1985.

When they saw this beautiful dove-shaped cloud formed by an Order of Angels just before their wedding, RA-Ja and Moi-RA knew their union was blessed by the Spirit.

RA-Ja and Moi-RA visited her home in the Philippines a few months after their wedding. Despite their difference in human age, their souls have been together from the beginning of time.

Lois East, a fine artist whose work has been published nationally, now devotes her talent to painting portraits of the beautiful angels she envisions. She and her husband Clay proudly admit that they were "brought together by the Angels."

Lois painted this angelic
being when she first
began meditating.

Pastel portraits by Lois East
of the angels, Treeaea and
Aereleas, finished in the
summer of 1994.

"Nancy," Nurse Brown said in a gentle, re-assuring voice, "you were here alone when I arrived. No one was in this room except you and . . . Kathy."

As if in a dream, Nancy stood staring at the body of her sweet, loving, shy daughter. For a split second, she thought that she saw the nurse's aide, Ian, looking at her from across the room. Then he seemed to disappear. That was when she was overcome by a soft, tranquil sense of peace.

The clock at Kathy's bedside had stopped at 3:31 P.M.

Twelve

A Message of Love

According to a basic theological consensus, humans do not become angels when they die. Angels are a host of cosmic beings who were created before our own earthly species. The Bible informs us that we are "a little lower than the angels" on the rungs of the spiritual ladder, but for some reason not totally clear to us, the Angels of Love seem intent upon helping us climb up to a higher level.

While I take careful note of the above-mentioned theological points regarding the nature of our angelic guides, I have a number of cases in my research files in which the spirits of the departed have—at least for a time—maintained a loving proprietary interest in their Earth-plane love partners.

* * *

When her husband died in the fall of 1944, Dorothy Barnes of Vermont found herself beset with the many problems that a widow inherits upon the death of her mate.

Since she had two children under four years of age, Dorothy's most immediate problem had to do with finding enough money to keep them all eating. Her husband had left only a miniscule estate, as far as his insurance policies went, but he had bequeathed her a section of timberland.

"A certain gentleman from the community made me an offer which seemed fair to me," Dorothy said. "I knew that he had a reputation for pulling some rather slick deals, but I didn't think that he would try to take advantage of a young widow."

In his last days, as he had lain dying of cancer of the stomach, her husband Phil had been unable to sleep at night. In those restless and painful hours, he would lie at Dorothy's side and gently stroke her hair.

The night before she was to close the deal on the timberland, she lay in a light sleep, mentally debating the wisdom of her actions.

"I had not been sleeping long," she recalled, "when I became conscious of a hand stroking my hair. I knew then that Phil was still watching over me—and I felt prepared to handle any situation."

Dorothy awakened totally convinced that she should not sell the property.

"I found out later that just the timber on the land was worth more than the price that the man had offered me for the entire property."

The young widow struggled for over a year, trying her best to make ends meet.

After sixteen months, she was forced to the painful consideration that it might be better for all of them if she boarded her children temporarily and set out alone to get a good job in a larger city. To do so would be to increase her opportunities to make enough money so that they could all be reunited as soon as possible with fewer financial problems.

Dorothy found a young couple in a nearby town who had six or seven children already boarding with them and who seemed to be the ideal kind of temporary foster parents for her two small children. She made all necessary arrangements with the man and woman, and all that remained for her to do was to deliver her kids to them early the next morning.

"That night, as before, when I had been undecided about the sale of the land, I felt my husband's steady hand gently caressing my hair," Dorothy said.

"I awoke with the utmost certainty that I must not leave my children with that young couple. I knew that I must not go ahead with my plans to board them."

Only a few weeks later, Dorothy read in the newspaper that the couple had been arrested for ill-treating the children in their care and for feeding them spoiled food.

Four years after her husband's death, Dorothy found herself in a position wherein she was seriously considering remarriage.

"It was no secret that Bob indulged in more than a social nip, but he seemed quite able to handle his drink. Oh, I had seen him drunk on more than one occasion, but I rationalized this by saying that everyone got a little tipsy once in a while."

She had nearly made up her mind to say "yes" to Bob's entreaties, when, one night, she again felt the soft caress of her dead husband's hand.

Dorothy changed her plans, reluctantly at first. Then she experienced the knee-weakening sensation of a narrow escape. Bob's father called her to confess and to warn her that Bob was an alcoholic who had already spent one expensive session of many months' duration in a hospital.

"I later found out that Phil's seemingly ever-vigilant spirit was not really jealous or possessive of me," Dorothy wrote in her account of her experiences.

"For a time there, I thought that his presence would never allow me to marry, that his caressing hand would always materialize to find fault with any man who courted me—but such was not at all the case.

"I have now been happily married for over twenty years. The beloved ghost of my first husband was only looking after me like a guardian angel until he could safely leave me to fend for myself."

When Michele Walinski's husband Andrew died, she left the East Coast and moved to California, selling nearly everything she owned in the process.

For more than a year she was unable to obtain any kind of steady employment. Then, finally, she decided to reactivate some long-dormant skills, and she found work as a laboratory technician in a small medical clinic.

Four years later, after she had successfully re-established herself as a highly effective technician, one of the doctors, who had recently obtained a divorce from his second wife, began to court Michele in sudden earnest.

Michele had always considered the doctor to be charming, but she had never felt entirely at ease with him. She was astonished and nonplussed when, after their third date, he asked her to marry him.

The longer they dated, the more that Michele doubted that she could ever really love the man, but he became even more persistent in his entreaties for her to marry him.

After stalling him for another two months— and after a great deal of mental debate— she at last accepted his proposal of marriage.

One night, shortly before their wedding date, Michele, unable to get to sleep, sat up in her bed reading.

"After a while, I noticed a strange radiation around the typewriter that I had left on a desk across the room," she stated in her report to me.

"I glanced about my bedroom, trying to discover what could be casting such a peculiar glow on that particular spot.

"I tried to get back to my reading, but I kept finding myself strangely attracted to that glowing blob of light.

"Then I heard the sound of typewriter keys being struck— slowly, methodically."

Michele said that she got out of bed and walked toward the desk.

"When I was only a few feet from the typewriter, I was able to see quite clearly the image of my late husband Andrew seated before the keyboard. I raised a hand as if to touch him—then he and the illumination disappeared."

She turned on the light, removed the sheet of paper from the typewriter.

"The spirit of my husband had typed these words: 'Don't marry Doctor. He will cause you heartbreak, pain, sorrow.'"

Confused, troubled by the incredible manifestation of her dead husband, Michele told her fiancé that she needed more time to think things over before she made the ultimate commitment. She asked that the wedding be postponed.

The doctor reluctantly agreed to her terms, but their relationship soon became more than a little strained.

Then, within a few months, the doctor killed himself in a fit of despondency over heavy gambling debts. Although he had somehow managed to keep it a secret from his colleagues in the clinic, the doctor had been a compulsive gambler.

The orthodox psychologist may assess Michele Walinski's account as being the fantasy of a lonely woman who feared the re-establishment of an intimate relationship with a man.

Others may suggest that the so-called spirit writing of her deceased husband was but Michele Walinski's own automatic writing in which she unconsciously typed out her inner fears.

But Michele herself will always believe that her husband's love had survived the grave and had enabled him to return to warn her of an inadvisable union with a man who would truly have caused her "heartbreak, pain, and sorrow."

Part Three

Angels of Love: Gentle Guides of Destiny

Thirteen

Mirrors of Their
Angels' Love

The December 27, 1993 issue of *Newsweek* magazine ran a cover story on the popular interest in angels— an interest that extended far beyond the Christmas holiday. Among the individuals cited as those who had received personal angelic encounters was Lori Jean Flory, and I read the paragraph referring to her experiences with great interest: ". . . Lori Jean Flory, 36, of Aurora, Colo., has been experiencing angels since the age of 3 . . . Usually they appear as light in motion with a vaguely human shape, and the message is always the same: 'They want us to know our pure essence is pure light and pure love.' "

Destiny will often arrange things perfectly. It was not more than a few weeks after reading this article and the reference to Ms. Flory when Lori Jean wrote to Sherry and me and initiated what has proven to be a most delightful friendship.

When I told Lori Jean about my book project retelling the accounts of angels bringing sweethearts and spouses together, she told us that she and her husband Charles had been brought together by her special angelic guide, Daephrenocles. According to Lori Jean, Daephrenocles told her, "We angels would have pulled you around until you came together— no matter how long it would take."

Early in 1980, the year after she had graduated from California Lutheran College, she was told the following during a telephone call from a psychically gifted friend named Kathy, who lived in southern California:

"Your true love is coming. He is not here yet. Right now he is involved with someone, and he is growing spiritually. He is learning specific lessons, as is the woman with whom he is currently involved. You are growing and learning lessons as well. When your true love comes, you will feel like following him wherever he goes.

"Do not run after the first man that you

meet that you might think is he. If you rush a relationship, there will be a divorce. If you learn your lessons, you will meet him when you are twenty-five. If you do not learn your lessons, you will not meet him until he is fifty."

At the time that Lori Jean received the psychic impression from Kathy, she had just begun to date Jim, a man that she had met while working for a woman who ran a dating agency in Turlock, California.

"Admittedly, I still had much to learn about life and had much growing to do," Lori Jean said. "I was finding out that it was not easy supporting myself during my first year out of college.

"Jim had recently broken off with a woman to whom he had been engaged. When he got a job in San Diego, he asked me if I wanted to move down there with him. I was living at the time with two female housemates in Turlock. Jim spent two months in San Diego by himself, and then I moved down to join him."

After Lori Jean had been living with Jim for a while, her friend Kathy predicted that on December 19 she would be given a wondrous surprise from the angels.

"December 19, 1982 came and went, and I

thought nothing more of my 'wondrous surprise' from the angels. I had forgotten that there is no time or space in the spiritual realms and that the angels are often one year off in their timing."

Charitably, Lori Jean said that she and Jim grew through much karma together. They were married in September of 1982.

"As I look back, it would have been better if we had never married, but obviously we both had lessons to learn."

Lori Jean said that in June of 1983, she and Jim had moved from San Diego to the foothills of the Sierra Nevada Mountains in an effort to see if country living might not be a good change for them. It did not and Lori recalled feeling in danger from Jim's inability to control his fits of anger.

"I wish I had known then about co-dependence and dysfunction what I know now—but anyway, we moved to a beautiful area called Squaw Valley, near the entrance to Sequoia National Park. I had been used to metaphysical groups being readily accessible in San Diego. In the Fresno area, I was unable to meet anyone who had metaphysical beliefs.

"One day I phoned a woman minister back in Turlock to ask if she could suggest any like-minded individuals in the Fresno area. Even though she did not know it at the time, my relationship with Jim was coming to an end, and the angels were guiding her to direct me to my first meeting with Charles Flory, my present husband. She referred me to George Gillette, a psychic reader, and Charles, an astrologer, who were sharing an office. I called George and made an appointment with him."

On the appointed day, August 10, 1983, Lori Jean drove to Clovis, a suburb of Fresno, for her reading with George Gillette. It was a hot day, and she had her hair pulled back in a ponytail.

"I don't know why I didn't just go walking right into the office as any normal person would do, but for some reason I just opened the door a crack and kind of slowly peeked in. Charles was sitting at the front desk, and he asked if he could help me. Sometimes I am a little on the shy side, especially if I don't know someone.

"While George was finishing with a client, I told Charles how happy I was to find some people in the area who were open to metaphysical things."

One month later, her relationship with Jim had deteriorated beyond any hope of salvation. Then, one September evening, Lori had to make her decision.

"By this time, we were sleeping in separate rooms. I told Jim that I was leaving the next day and that I did not plan to return. Jim didn't believe me. Up to that point, I had been too embarrassed to tell anyone what had been going on in our marriage— especially since the wedding had been a very expensive one. But I called my father, and told him [about our troubles.] Dad told me to pack up my things right away and to come home."

Lori Jean packed up as much as she could into her car, including a kitten and two puppies, and left for her parents' home on September 10, 1983.

"As pulled into Fresno, the brakes on my car failed. Thank goodness I wasn't going very fast and there was a mechanic right across the street.

"In spite of all the terrible things that I had been through, I still felt grateful for all the protection that the angels had given me. After all, I was still alive!"

Lori Jean lived with her parents for two weeks.

"Bless their hearts. Some of the stories I told them about my married life almost made their hair stand up on end. I thank God for their support."

We've got your authors!

If you seek out the latest historical romances by today's bestselling authors, our new reader's service, KENSINGTON CHOICE, is the club for you.

KENSINGTON CHOICE is the only club where you can find authors like Janelle Taylor, Shannon Drake, Rosanne Bittner, Sylvie Sommerfield, Penelope Neri and Phoebe Conn all in one place...

...and the only service that will deliver their romances direct to your home as soon as they are published—even before they reach the bookstores.

KENSINGTON CHOICE is also the only service that will give you a substantial guaranteed discount off the publisher's price on every one of those romances.

That's right: Every month, the Editors at Zebra and Pinnacle select four of the newest novels by our bestselling authors and rush them straight to you, usually *before they reach the bookstores*. The publisher's prices for these romances range from $4.99 to $5.99—but they are always yours for the guaranteed low price of just *$4.20!*

That means you'll always save over 20%...often as much as 30%...off the publisher's prices on every shipment you get from KENSINGTON CHOICE!

All books are sent on a 10-day free examination basis, and there is no minimum number of books to buy. (A postage and handling charge of $1.50 is added to each shipment.)

As your introduction to the convenience and value of this new service, we invite you to accept

4 BOOKS FREE

The 4 books, worth up to $23.96, are our welcoming gift. You pay only $1 to help cover postage and handling.

To start your subscription to KENSINGTON CHOICE and receive your introductory package of 4 FREE romances, detach and mail the postpaid card at right *today*.

We have 4 FREE BOOKS for you as your introduction to KENSINGTON CHOICE
To get your FREE BOOKS, worth up to $23.96, mail the card below.

FREE BOOK CERTIFICATE

As my introduction to your new KENSINGTON CHOICE reader's service, please send me 4 FREE historical romances (worth up to $23.96), billing me just $1 to help cover postage and handling. As a KENSINGTON CHOICE subscriber, I will then receive 4 brand-new romances to preview each month for 10 days FREE. I can return any shipment within 10 days and owe nothing. The publisher's prices for the KENSINGTON CHOICE romances range from $4.99 to $5.99, but as a subscriber I will be entitled to get them for just $4.20 per book or $16.80 for all four titles. There is no minimum number of books to buy, and I can cancel my subscription at any time. A $1.50 postage and handling charge is added to each shipment.

Name _____

Address _____ Apt. _____

City _____ State _____ Zip _____

Telephone ( ) _____

Signature _____

(If under 18, parent or guardian must sign)

Subscription subject to acceptance. Terms and prices subject to change.

KC0195

We have
4
FREE
Historical
Romances
for you!

(worth up
to $23.96!)

Details inside!

KENSINGTON CHOICE
Reader's Service
120 Brighton Road
P.O.Box 5214
Clifton, NJ 07015-5214

A restraining order was filed against Jim, and Lori Jean worked at getting on with her life. She got a job teaching preschool in Fresno— and she turned twenty-five.

"Although my pets helped so much with my healing process, my landlady eventually said that either they had to go— or I did. At the time it nearly broke my heart to have to give them up, but now I can see that all of these 'releases' and 'clearances' were preparing more space for Charles.

"At this time, though, Charles and I were only friendly acquaintances. He had no idea of most of the things that I was going through. But I seemed to keep encountering Charles all over the place— and always unexpectedly.

"In November, I filed for divorce through a friend of Dad's, who specialized in that area of law."

In early December, Lori Jean decided to visit a local nightspot "just to watch everyone else." After she had left Jim, even grocery shopping was an adventure, as there was no longer anyone to tell her what to do and to inform her that she was doing everything wrong.

"All of a sudden, who should I see but Charles and his date. I called out his name, and when he walked over to me, my mouth just took over my mind. I took both of his hands in mine and looked at his date with a very serious expression on my face. 'Look,' I told her, 'this man is special! You had better be good to him— or *you* are going to hear from *me!*'

"She just looked at me and didn't say a thing. The two of them left, and I thought to myself, 'Oh, God, what have I said?' "

Lori Jean later found out that that was Charles's only date with that woman. He also told Lori Jean that he had tried to ditch the lady and return to find her, but Lori Jean had already left.

"When we reflect on those early days of our budding relationship, Charles will often say that he was totally amazed that someone would say something like I did about him in someone else's presence. I am even *more* amazed that I had said such a thing. It was as though the angels were speaking and not me."

Lori Jean continued to run into Charles at the grocery store, the bank, and numerous other places. She was troubled that he now seemed uncomfortable in her presence. What she did not know at that time was that Charles was attracted to her, but that he was separated from his wife Leslie and he needed to bring that chapter of his life to a close.

* * *

As Christmas approached, Lori Jean decided to write down all of her feelings about Charles.

"It took me two pages to get everything down, and then I decided to do something daring. I would call Charles and read my feelings to him over the telephone. If he rejected me, well, at least I had expressed myself and I could move on.

"The next morning I called him at his office at 10:00 A.M. and we talked for two hours. Charles did not reject me, but he did admit that he was surprised to learn how I felt about him.

"That's when I realized that the date was *December 19*. My psychic friend Kathy had said that I would receive a wondrous gift from the angels on December 19. While I had looked for the blessing in 1982, the angels had just been a year off in our time reference."

As the days went by, Lori Jean learned that Charles had been attracted to her for quite some time and that he would have pursued her more actively if it had not been for his uncertain marital situation.

"By then, Jim and I were going through the process of divorce, and Charles and Leslie, who had separated so many times, had seen their marriage crash and burn. It can never be said that either of us broke up the other's marriage. We had managed to do that individually, all by ourselves."

Shortly before Christmas, there was a knock at Lori Jean's front door. Her roommate, Thelma, was asleep, so she had to answer it.

"There was Charles on the porch with a Christmas card in his hand. I asked him to come in, and I asked him if I didn't get a Christmas kiss. He wasted not a moment of time in obliging my request.

"We went to my room and we talked . . . and kissed some more. Nothing more than that. I had a Teddy bear that looked like a little football player, and I wanted Charles to have that for Christmas.

"After a couple of hours, he said that he thought that he had better be going. As he stepped out on the porch to leave, I looked at him and said, 'I feel honored and privileged to be standing here with you.'

"Charles said that he felt the same way— and from then on we began to see much more of one another."

On January 13, 1984, Lori Jean was visiting Charles in his office. It did not take long to determine that he was very upset with Leslie. He felt that Lori Jean should leave, but suddenly she received a signal that the angels wished to speak to Charles.

"Although Charles is a professional astrologer, he had never met spirit guides or angels. The angels had me ask him to have his chair face me and to have our knees touching. Next, they instructed him to touch my fingers very lightly.

"I took the time to relax, to breathe deeply, and to lift my consciousness. Then I simply let go and allowed the words to come through.

"The angels told Charles that it was time for him to get on with his life and to stop allowing himself to be abused and manipulated. It was time to feel good about his work and to tolerate no longer those who made fun of him.

"They went on to tell him that it was purely time to begin loving himself and to stop the suffering that he had been feeling. He was to free himself from the pain that he had endured that dated back before Leslie, to his first wife Kathy.

"The angels did not tell him what to do, they simply made suggestions to stop the suffering that he had been feeling for so long.

"The angelic energies were peaceful and

harmonious, and when I opened my eyes and looked at Charles's face, I could see that his troubled expression had turned to one of peace. Although I had been receiving the angelic vibrations since I was three years old, this was the first formal reading that I had ever given to anyone."

Charles asked her to remain in her chair and not to go anywhere. He left his office door open and went to the receptionist's desk to make a telephone call. No one was in the office except for his partner, George Gillette, and Lori Jean.

"Charles called Leslie and quite clearly and decisively told her that he wanted a divorce—and that this time he was not going to change his mind.

"He came back into the office with a relieved look on his face. He announced that he was going for lunch, and he asked if I wanted to go with him.

"So that was our first date. Charles loves English fish and chips, so we went out to have lunch. I was a little nervous, as it had been awhile since I had been on any kind of positive, loving date. I didn't quite know what to say or do or how to act—but it was fun! Charles still thanks the angels for that day of release."

* * *

Not long after that day, Lori Jean informed Charles that she felt he was going to be her second husband.

"Does that bother you?" she asked him.

"No," he said. "It certainly does not."

From then on, the two spent every day together.

"We literally could not get enough of each other. We jokingly complained that our bodies were getting in the way of our being as close as we really wanted to be. On the soul level, you see, we remembered merging our energies in the spirit state."

Then came the glorious day when Lori Jean visited Charles's office and was astonished when he unexpectedly got down on one knee and said: "I, Charles, love and serve you."

Lori Jean immediately followed suit and did the same thing for him.

"I have a box full of everything sentimental that we have ever given each other," Lori Jean said. "Once Charles gave me a card in which he had drawn two stick figures with a line connecting their hearts. He wrote that this connection between us would be like a rubber band that could stretch to any length— and that we would always be connected.

"One night after going to a meditation group, Charles dropped me off at Thelma's house; and before I got out of the car, he started to cry. He told me that nothing was wrong. They were happy tears because we were together."

The end of January, they went looking for an apartment and moved in together. They were in tune with one another from the very beginning. When they were out shopping separately, they would often come home to discover that they had brought each other the same gift.

They moved to Colorado together in October of 1984, and they were married in a Unity Church on July 28, 1985.

"My angel guide Daephrenocles says that Charles and I are like two white horses prancing together. He says that we are like 10 x 10 and not 1 + 1. We are doing our spiritual work together, and we work as a team.

"After more than ten years together, we are still very much in love. The words in our house are 'us, ours, and we,' not 'I, me, and you.'"

On June 18, 1994, Lori Jean and Charles were in the process of moving to a new home in Colorado at an even higher elevation, but she wrote to inform us that she had received confirmation that their recently acquired property was surrounded by a force-field of light.

"When I am relaxed," she said, "I see beyond the physical reality. I see the frequencies, energies, vibrations around us, and they are always of a high nature."

Years ago, Lori Jean learned that her angel guide Daephrenocles' personal symbol was a cross of light. As a Light Being from the eighth dimension, she has seen him manifest tiny crosses of light as a signal to the nature spirits that their property is off limits to them, as far as damage from nature is concerned.

"I have seen hail revert back to rain in moments when I have prayed that the flowers we love not be damaged. Charles and I hold nature to be sacred. Sadly, I have often seen our neighbors' property sustain damage from weather— yet ours has received none. They shake their heads and wonder why."

On this particular day in June, a tornado siren awakened Lori Jean from an afternoon nap.

"I immediately asked for protection, and I saw a brilliant flash of light at the foot of the bed.

"I looked out over our property, and I saw hundreds of clear, see-through etheric crosses of white light *everywhere*. Then I beheld the transparent light bodies of Higher Beings around the place.

"The wind became a breeze. The thunder calmed to silence. A gentle rain began to fall through breaking clouds. The threat of a tornado was no more. We were safe."

Fourteen

The Universal Language of the Soul

I have known Joshua Shapiro for many years, but I had not had the opportunity to meet Vera, his bride of six months, until Sherry and I joined Joshua on the lecture platform in Chicago in January of 1992.

Vera proved to be a very charming lady, and it was immediately apparent to Sherry and me that these two lightworkers had most certainly been brought together by the Angels of Love. The Shapiros agreed— and explained that since Vera was a native of Brazil, spirit had led Joshua on quite an odyssey in order to find his destiny.

* * *

Joshua pointed out that their story really began in 1989 when he was living in Pacifica, California, working for the city of Berkeley as a computer programmer.

"At the time, I was involved with a number of women," Joshua said, "but there wasn't anyone who was special. I was following my Aries nature in being independent and not being tied down."

In January or February of 1989, Joshua met Carmen Balehistero, a Brazilian channel for the entity of St. Germain. Ms. Balehistero had expressed an interest in the bizarre archaeological artifacts known as the "crystal skulls," and since Joshua was co-author with Sandra Bowen and Nick Nocerino of a book entitled *Mysteries of the Crystal Skulls,* the two found that they had a great deal to discuss.

It was during the course of that meeting that Carmen informed Joshua that she and her family were in charge of a spiritual group called Pax Universal that organized metaphysical conferences in Brazil. Joshua accepted her invitation to be a speaker at a conference in São Paulo in June of 1990.

Vera explained that 1989 had been a year of great changes in her life. A native of Brazil who had lived all of her life in São Paulo, the largest city in that country, she went to Peru for the first time in July of 1989 as part of a metaphysical tour led by her spiritual teacher Luiz Gasparetto, a famous psychic. In Vera's opinion, the experiences which she underwent in Peru changed her life completely.

"While we visited the ancient mountain city of Machu Picchu in Peru," Vera said, "Gasparetto channeled an entity named Chuma, who said that she had been a high priestess of the Inca. She gave us the true history of Machu Picchu as well as specific information about some of the people in our group."

When she returned to Brazil, Vera herself received a message from the entity Chuma.

"She told me that I should quit my nice-paying job as manager of a large bank. Chuma said that I should begin organizing tours to Peru that would provide individuals with the opportunity for spiritual experiences at the various powerful energy vortexes that exist in that country."

Vera was cautious. "I was very confused about this inner message from Chuma. I am a Virgo. I don't just make changes in my life on a whim. I felt a great deal of fear about making such a dramatic change to do work that I had never done before."

Vera told us that she asked the spirit teacher for signs that would clearly demonstrate to her that such work was truly to be her life's path.

"I did receive several proofs, but the most powerful and convincing one came through Gasparetto when he was in the trance state and channeling artwork from some of the great masters.

"I prayed inwardly and told Chuma that if one of the artists who channeled through Gasparetto should paint her face, then I would absolutely believe in her message."

After the session was completed, the psychic's assistant showed the observers all the many paintings that various entities had channeled through Gasparetto.

"In one of the pictures was the face of a high priestess that I immediately recognized as Chuma," Vera recalled. "It was the same face that I saw in meditation when she communicated with me.

"I walked closer to the painting and I saw that Chuma's name was written on the canvas. The work had been signed by Toulouse-Lautrec. My heart began to beat very fast, and from that day on I have never questioned Chuma's messages. I quit my job at the bank; and thirty days later, I was on board on airplane to Peru with my first tour group."

***

Joshua remembered that in April of 1989 he had developed an unexplainable compulsion to go to Peru.

"Although I couldn't explain *why* I had to go to Peru, I have learned over the years to trust the inner voice."

He met with Peter Schneider, President of Peru Mystic Tours in Lima, while he was visiting in San Francisco.

"Peter has a strong interest in the UFO phenomenon, and he had attended a UFO sharing group which I had hosted in my home. He said that he could help me with his agency, and even said that I could stay in his home in Lima."

In December of 1989, Joshua visited Machu Picchu, Cuzco, and Lake Titicaca.

"I was especially drawn to Lake Titicaca as I had heard reports of a secret brotherhood in the area. While there, I had a spiritual reading from a shaman who lived on the Island of Amantani. He used coca leaves in his reading. He would throw them in the air and chant in what seemed to be a combination of Spanish and Quecha, the native language of the Inca. Depending upon where and how the leaves landed, the shaman would gain information about myself or the question I had asked."

When Joshua asked if he would ever be married, the medicine man answered, "Yes, to a Peruvian woman."

Intrigued by such a prediction, Joshua's thoughts moved back in time to a conference that he had attended earlier that year. He had found himself gazing at a Hispanic woman, and his inner voice had told him that one day he would be involved with such a woman.

Joshua recalled that the shaman's prophecy had sent a feeling "like electricity" running through his body.

"But what this meant at the time, I really didn't know; for I had never been involved with a Hispanic woman before."

Vera's first tour to mystical Peru had been a great success— but then she was forced to deal with the reality of the rainy season. She really could not offer tours during the period of December to March.

"This caused me to become very depressed," she told us. "I began to question again if offering tours to Peru was really the right thing for me to do since I didn't have any other source of income at that time."

An elderly teacher from a sacred spiritual society guided her through a special ritual in which she placed a tall mirror against a wall and sat before it with a white candle in her hands. The teacher told her to focus her entire attention on the light.

"After I went into a trance state, I didn't see myself any longer in the mirror. I saw a strange, but familiar, young woman about twenty years old. She was dressed in old Peruvian clothes, and she had long dark hair and was very pretty. I heard the smiling woman tell me that everything in my life would be all right. The feelings that I received from her were strength, confidence, freedom, happiness, and peace."

When the teacher who was guiding Vera through the experience asked the pretty young woman in the mirror what she meant when she said everything would be all right, Vera began to perceive different images above the woman's head.

"It was like watching a movie of a past time in Machu Picchu. I knew that the woman was me in a past life when I lived in the ancient city as an Inca.

"I saw her sitting on a large stone in Machu Picchu. A man approached her and they began to hug and to kiss. I knew the woman was me, but I did not recognize the face of the man.

"Then the movie changed. The man was crying, saying that he had to leave. She was understanding of his need to go, but she asked, 'What about our child?' And the only thing that I could understand from the man was that he felt he had no choice other than to leave the relationship."

As Vera watched these images, she talked out loud to share everything with her teacher-guide.

"He helped me to ask the questions, to better understand their situation. They seemed to ignore me— even though I was certain that they were aware of me.

"My teacher advised me to return to the face of the woman and the mirror, and it felt like we were linked together for hours. I was in utter joy, experiencing her essence and all her feelings and emotions.

"Naturally there was a part of me that was concerned that I was remaining too long in trance, but it was so wonderful to be with this other part of me that I couldn't let her go. My friend and teacher understood and told me to take my time. So I stayed at the mirror until she disappeared.

"Once the ritual was over, I rejoiced in the wonderfulness of the experience, but I still didn't feel that I had any real answers— so my depression was still inside of me."

Ten days after he returned from Peru in December of 1989, Joshua had an opportunity to move to Las Vegas to work with friends to create a non-profit New Age foundation.

On May 3, 1990, he was walking down a main street in Las Vegas, heading for a restaurant at lunchtime, when he heard a loud screech directly behind him.

"My last remembrance was everything blacking out, from bottom to top. The next thing I remember is waking up in a hospital, strapped down to a bed. I found out that it was two days later.

"I was asked if I could recall the truck that had struck me. At first I thought the doctor was joking, but then I was informed that a van had jumped the sidewalk curb and had struck me. I had a scrape on my left ankle, but no broken bones. I felt very weak and had little energy, but I never really experienced being hit by the van. To this day, I believe that some higher intelligence took my spirit out of my body and traveled with me to inner dimensions. I have a distinct feeling that I attended some kind of important meeting, but I have no clear memory of this time.

"I flew to Colorado about two weeks after the accident, and it seemed to me that I had been on some kind of flying vehicle during the two days that I was in a coma."

By the end of May, Joshua was able to get around with little difficulty; and he continued with his plans to leave to speak at the Brazilian metaphysical conference in June.

He missed his plane in Los Angeles, because no one had informed him that he needed a visa to travel to Brazil. He rescheduled his first presentation for two days later, and when he arrived in São Paulo, he was overwhelmed by the interest that he received from the local media. Then he learned that he would be speaking to an audience of three thousand people.

"The first day I spoke about UFOs and the second about the crystal skulls," Joshua said. "I really fell in love with Brazil and its people. I felt very comfortable being with them."

About the middle of December 1989, Vera sought out the services of a highly recommended psychic, in an effort to gain more insights into her uncertain life.

"I remember sitting in the woman's living room when she opened the door, walked directly over to me, smiled, and hugged me, saying, 'Oh, I can see that you finally discovered your mission in this lifetime!'

"I felt very strange— and I wondered what she was talking about."

Vera accompanied the psychic into her "special room" where the woman used a deck of regular playing cards to accomplish her consultations.

"She told me that I was finally reconnecting with my past and that I should trust the choice that I had made. She said that my mission in this lifetime was to take people to Peru to assist them in recognizing their Inca lifetimes. I was very impressed with this woman because her words were so accurate without my saying one word or asking one question."

Vera finally asked the psychic how she could know all those things that she was telling her.

The psychic smiled and replied: "When I look at you, I see the priestess that you were in Peru. You are a very special soul. You have a mission to accomplish. You should not worry, because the universe will take care of everything for you. Continue to conduct your tours. You have made the correct choice. Be peaceful about it."

And then the woman's consultation went an entirely different direction.

"I know that you are very happy being single and that you don't want to get married," she told Vera. "But I need to tell you that in the first six months of the next year [1990], you are going to meet your soulmate."

The psychic went on, telling the astonished Vera that everything between her and this man would happen so fast that she would not have time to think about it. Everything was being arranged in the higher dimensions between Vera and this man, whose name she believed to be Ricardo.

"By the time that you finally become conscious of what you are doing," the psychic explained to Vera, "you will be married to this man and living in another country."

Vera was totally frustrated. "There is no way in hell that I will leave my country to marry someone!"

Then she remembered that the psychic had teased her and said, "He is such a wonderful man that if you don't want him, give him *my* phone number!"

A few months later, Vera found herself taking a workshop on crystals conducted by Carmen Balehistero. During one of the classes, the topic suddenly changed to that of crystal skulls.

"When I heard those words, 'crystal skulls,' my heart jumped," Vera said. "Somehow I could no longer pay attention to anything else Carmen was saying for the rest of the class. I had thought that I knew everything there was to know about crystals— and now, suddenly, I was hearing about something new."

Later, after the class, Vera inquired further about the strange new topic.

Carmen told her that the mystery of crystal skulls was a subject area that would be covered at her next metaphysical conference.

"I met a man in San Francisco who is knowledgeable about the crystal skulls," Carmen said. "I hope to bring him here to lecture on the subject."

Vera told us that she could not stop thinking about crystal skulls and this man that Carmen hoped to bring to Brazil.

"After the workshop, I saw Carmen three or four times before the conference, and she finally told me that the man had confirmed that he would be coming to Brazil to speak about the crystal skulls," Vera said. "She added that I should watch television in the next few days because she would be showing a video that she had on the subject."

Vera was seated excitedly before her television set on the Saturday night when the program would show the video on crystal skulls.

"I became hypnotized by the magic of the crystal skulls," she remembered. "The different poses of the skulls in tandem with the background music was very powerful. As if I were in a trance, I could see flashes of my past lives— pyramids, Mayans, Atlantis, UFOs.

"However, this video did not contain any verbal information, so it only made me all the more excited to meet this man from the United States who would be bringing all this information to Brazil."

The Third International Metaphysical Conference sponsored by Pax Universal was held from June 29 to July 1, 1990. Vera was a volunteer at the conference, but she managed to be in the front row when Joshua Shapiro gave his presentation on crystal skulls.

"I was totally fascinated with all the information that Joshua shared—just as everyone else in the room was," Vera said. "The room was very quiet, as people had to wait for Carmen to translate his English into Portuguese.

"During Joshua's presentation something very interesting happened to me. I was sitting next to a blind man and all of a sudden an extraterrestrial entity appeared in front of me. The entity came close to my ear and said, 'Vera, do you remember the library that Chuma mentioned when you were in Peru? The library *is* a crystal skull!'

"And I said, 'Oh, now I understand!' When I was in Peru, Chuma told us that when the human beings were ready, they would find a library in Machu Picchu that will reveal the science of life—the past, the present, and the future.

"I had not understood the entity Chuma at the time, but now I perceived that the information of the great library was in the crystal skull and would not be damaged because crystal is a hard substance that could remain buried and unharmed in the ground of Machu Picchu for a long time.

"The blind man sitting next to me leaned over and whispered, 'What is Shapiro talking about? A library in Machu Picchu?'

"And then I laughed, because he couldn't *see* the entity that had spoken to me, but he had *heard* him! The blind man was confused, because he couldn't tell if Joshua was saying this or someone else—the entity—was speaking."

Vera remembered that when Joshua concluded his presentation, he commented that if anyone had had any kind of an experience during his presentation about the crystal skull to please come forward to speak to him about it.

"I thought at the time that I should share this information about the library with him, but I didn't know any English, so I decided to forget it.

"I knew that there was to be a party on the last day of the conference. Joshua would be likely to be there. Perhaps if the situation arose, I might be able to mention it to him there."

* * *

Joshua remembered having a wonderful time at the party for the conference speakers and organizers. Although he did not speak Portuguese, there were enough Brazilians there who spoke good English.

"A woman named Dulce told me that she had a friend who wanted to speak with me about an experience that she had during my presentation at the conference," he said. "But for some reason I didn't seem to be able to get over to speak to the woman until the party was ending.

"I went up to Dulce, learned that her friend's name was Vera. We all agreed that the hour was getting late, so courtesy dictated that I be polite and express a hope that we might have an opportunity to talk before I needed to return to the United States."

In retrospect, Joshua told us, he has since wondered why he didn't feel an immediate connection with Vera.

"And Vera has since told me that although she was fascinated with the information that I shared about the crystal skull, she didn't really like my spontaneous and somewhat lighthearted lecture style."

The next day, a Monday, Joshua and the other speakers from the United States went to the home of a famous Brazilian television producer to be interviewed regarding their special areas of expertise. Vera was also there, still wishing to tell him about her experience during his presentation on the crystal skulls.

"Pepe, Vera's tour guide in Peru, had been one of the speakers at the conference, so he was able to translate for us while we drove to the producer's home. I saw that a healer who had offered to 'balance' Vera's energy had only made her dizzy and confused, so while we were waiting in the producer's garden to be interviewed, I offered to help restore her psychic equilibrium."

After Joshua had finished restoring Vera's energy to a better balance, he felt strongly that he had known her before in a previous life experience.

"Her energy was very familiar. Somehow, a special connection was established between us— or perhaps we were reactivating a connection from our past. I felt that we had been married before, and I told her this."

When it came time for Joshua's interview, Vera also recorded it on his video camera.

"Later, I remember that we held hands all the way back to the hotel."

Joshua joined Vera, her roommate, and Pepe for dinner; and afterwards, he and Vera went down to her car in the garage to talk privately. Also, it was Vera's assignment as a conference volunteer to see to it that Joshua got back to his hotel that night.

"Well," Joshua smiled, "one thing led to another, and I never returned to my hotel room that night."

Vera attended the after-conference party with the expectation of being able to speak to Joshua about her experience during his presentation on the crystal skulls. However, her friend Dulce made three unsuccessful attempts to bring Joshua over to their table, so Vera had grown discouraged.

"Joshua was too busy talking with other people at the party. Carmen, the conference organizer left the party, then came back to speak with me. She asked me if I would be able to bring Pepe, my Peruvian guide, to be part of a television interview that was scheduled for the next day. I told her that I would be happy to help out."

Vera and Dulce were at the front door of the restaurant preparing to leave when Joshua finally came over to Dulce to ask about her friend.

"It was too late to talk with him; so I told Dulce to forget it, and we left."

To Vera's surprise, Joshua and some of the other speakers from the United States were waiting at the hotel for transportation to the producer's home. She asked Pepe to translate for her, and she was at last able to tell Joshua about her mystical experience during his presentation and about an earlier UFO encounter.

"I feel very strongly that something, some energy or force, made Carmen return to the party to ask that favor of me. If she hadn't come back to ask me to accompany the speakers who were to be interviewed that next day, I would not have had an opportunity to be with Joshua. Maybe an angel guided her."

At this time, Vera told us, she did not feel any special connection with Joshua nor any attraction to him as a man.

"When the healer had made me feel strange and dizzy, I was unsure whether I should accept Joshua's help. But I felt so bad that I gave him permission to work with me.

"I held his hands, closed my eyes, started to breathe— and I immediately left my body.

"I went back to the time in which I was the Inca woman in Machu Picchu. The same man was speaking to me and crying. Somehow I knew that the man who was with me in that Inca life was Joshua.

"When I returned to full consciousness, Joshua was asking me if I was okay. After I said that I was, he told me that he felt that we had known each other before. I thought, 'Oh, no, maybe he, too, went into a trance and saw that Inca time with me.'

"And when he said, 'You were my wife in a past life,' I thought for certain that he must have seen everything!

"Then he smiled in a funny way and said, 'You are going to marry me again in this lifetime!'

"I thought, 'Oh, my God! Americans are crazy! Forget it! No way!'"

Later, Vera recalled, the "magic" started to happen. Pepe, who had been translating for them, wasn't around anymore— and she and Joshua continued to speak to one another although neither understood the other's native tongue.

As they grew friendlier, the hours literally seemed to melt away.

"Joshua and I talked and talked until very late. We shared things about ourselves in a magical way. I would be saying something to him, and before I even completed my thought, he was completing it for me. And the same thing was happening for him. I knew what he was going to say and could complete his sentences.

"I still don't understand how two people who could not speak the other's language could do this. My only guess is that at this time the language of love was already speaking through us."

Joshua was supposed to stay in Brazil until the end of the week as he had a private lecture scheduled for the Pax Universal Center. A problem developed with the hotel in which Joshua was staying, so Carmen asked Vera if he might stay in her apartment until he returned to the United States. He immediately bought a Portuguese-English, English-Portuguese dictionary for each of them.

"I could not believe that I was speaking of marriage. I had been married once before. I wasn't certain that I would ever repeat the experience," Joshua recalled.

"One day when I was with Vera and a few friends in her apartment, I felt that our connection in the past life in Peru was so strong that I started crying. Normally, I don't get this emotional, but I was overcome with a joy of meeting her again. My tears were not of sadness, but of joy.

"When it was time for me to return to the United States, I knew that I had met a very special person, and I definitely planned to stay in touch with her."

* * *

After the "magic" had occurred between them, Vera was struck with the sad reality that Joshua would only be staying a few more days in Brazil.

"We really wanted to be together as much as possible," she said. "We had four days, and I wanted to make them last as if they were four years.

"When he left, Joshua told me that he felt for certain that we would be married. Even though our connection was *very strong,* I could not imagine how this could happen."

However, two days after Joshua had returned to the States, Vera's telephone rang—and there was the "crazy" American trying to speak Portuguese using the dictionary that he had bought in Brazil.

"I couldn't believe it! I knew that he would write to me, but there he was, live, on the telephone, speaking to me. I felt so bad that I couldn't speak English. When we had been together, we could feel what the other person was trying to say. We could read our thoughts and feelings through our eyes and gestures. But on the phone, it was impossible. I told Joshua to call in the morning. I had begun to take some English classes, and my teacher would be there to translate."

* * *

Back in the States, Joshua felt that he finally understood what the shaman had meant in Lake Titicaca when he had told him that he would marry a Peruvian woman. Even though Vera was Brazilian, she had told him that Machu Picchu in Peru was her true spiritual home.

It was indeed fortunate for Joshua and Vera that she had a friend who was teaching English and who could translate for them on the telephone.

"Vera was willing to help pay for my trip back to Brazil by organizing some lectures there for me. In addition, she was taking another group to Peru, and she invited me to go, free of charge. I charged my airfare on my credit card, and I was able to return to Brazil at the end of August, just before she took her group to Peru."

By the time that Joshua returned to Brazil in August, Vera said that she was more comfortable with the idea of marrying him.

In July, she had taken a tour group to Machu Picchu, and she had gone off by herself to do a meditation on Huyna Picchu, the mountain that overlooks the ancient Peruvian city.

"I placed a picture of Joshua on the ground, and I asked God and my guides to please help me to understand what the relationship with Joshua meant to my life. I needed to know what to do, because things were becoming very serious between our letters and our telephone conversations.

"As I was looking at the picture of Joshua, a butterfly flew over it— then stopped to rest on top of it. Incredibly, the butterfly stayed on his picture for fifteen minutes.

"I don't know how to explain this, but I felt that I was having a telepathic conversation with the butterfly. I was able to feel peace and confidence. And for the first time since I met Joshua, I felt secure in our relationship.

"The butterfly somehow was able to help me to release all my fears, doubts, and questions.

"I felt that the butterfly was like an angel who helped me to see the answers clearly.

"After this experience with the butterfly, I didn't hesitate to open my heart completely to Joshua.

"And before he left Brazil the second time, I accepted his invitation to come to the United States and marry him. And the psychic had been correct about my future husband being named 'Ricardo.' Although his spiritual name is Joshua, his birth name was 'Richard.' "

The September 1990 trip to Peru was really a time of celebration for Joshua and Vera as they had the opportunity to be together in the places where they had spent one of their most powerful past lifetimes. Joshua found that he was able to do a great deal of healing work and to channel energy to some of the people who were in their tour group. He could almost hear the spirit of the ancient Inca whispering to him.

"Our special memory of the trip was that we went back to the exact spot where Vera had conducted her meditation with the butterfly on Haynu Picchu, and we did a meditation together.

"Then, further up, near the top of the mountain, in the Temple of the Moon we conducted our own sacred spiritual marriage and promised to work together to do God's work."

Joshua explained that it took about three months for U.S. Immigration to approve a fiancée visa for Vera, and then another five months for the American Consulate in São Paulo to approve it. In July of 1991, Vera arrived in the United States.

"On September 7, almost exactly one year from the day that we performed our spiritual marriage in Machu Picchu, we were married near Chicago in a simple ceremony by a minister of the Church of Religious Science in one of the local parks.

Fifteen

The Wonderful Union of Twin Flames

I have known Moi-RA and RA-Ja Dove for many years now, and the all-prevailing impression that I have always received from them is that of love. They speak freely of their guidance from otherworldly and multi-dimensional beings, and they seem completely dedicated to their avowed goal of serving as beaconlights of peace, love, and light on Earth.

Although a superficial glance might initially focus upon the physical contrasts between a ruggedly built American man and a diminutive lady from the Philippines who is a few Earth-years older than he, the challenge is to comprehend that such mundane matters as appearance, age, and ethnicity have no bearing on the truth or the power of a spiritual message.

Moi-RA was born into a spiritualist family who lived in a small province near Manila in the Philippines. Her mother died when Moi-RA was only two, leaving her with her father, whom she grew later to consider the greatest philosopher she has ever known.

When she was four, Moi-RA heard her father tell her uncle, "This child of mine is an old soul. She is going to do something important for the world."

At that same age, Moi-RA's eldest sister took her to seances at the Spiritualist Center that had been founded by her uncle, Juan Ortega, the originator of the world famous trained Philippine Psychic Surgeons.

"I would sleep at the beginning of the sessions," Moi-Ra said, "but I would wake up automatically when my uncle would deliver spirit messages. I clearly remember being so interested in those messages, especially when he talked about the angels and outer space. Later, I discovered the same wisdom in the Theosophical Society of which I became a member at the age of sixteen."

Moi-RA kept to herself and seldom played with other children. "I loved to read stories about Buck Rogers in outer space from the comics section of the newspaper," she recalled. "I read books until sundown everyday. My father would look for me all over the house—and then find me hiding behind walls in a window overhang where I could watch the ocean and read to my heart's content."

An amazing spiritual experience occurred to Moi-RA during her teen years.

"It was during one full moon of May which is called the *Wesak* Festival, the time when the Buddha comes back to give his blessings to the Earth. According to tradition, the masters and teachers of humanity meet in the Wesak Valley during this time. I saw myself in a vision sitting on the top steps of an amphitheater that had been hewn from the ground. I felt a continuous stream of tiny droplets of cool refreshing mist enveloping my entire being, bringing a feeling of healing and a blessed calm of contentment and peace.

"Then I beheld the masters and the teachers arriving one by one, wearing flowing robes. I saw them form a six-pointed star on the grounds while the Buddha appeared in the night sky above the amphitheater, giving his blessings to the world.

"As member of the Esoteric Group in the Theosophical Society I was supposed to 'tune in to' this festival each year; but that year, in my vision, I actually attended it.

"Later in life, I made the practice become a physical reality by actually pilgrimaging to the Wesak Valley to worship in the holiness and to imbibe the wisdom of the Buddha."

All the time she spent reading certainly produced valuable academic dividends for the young woman. She became a superior student, pursuing advanced work after her college graduation and becoming a university professor of Ethics and the Religions of the Far East, as well as a Dean of Women and a guidance counselor.

In spite of her academic degrees, Moi-RA clung to her childhood belief that each person is led immediately to wed his or her soulmate.

"I married a man who quickly disproved my hypothesis, but I had four children by him. When I had the fourth, I nearly died. The anesthesiologist had sought to stop the operation because my pulse had touched bottom—but then quickly picked up again. The child, a girl, died six hours later. When I woke up, I knew what had happened even before the nurse told me."

Later, she was told that the surgery had taken nearly three hours. Amazingly, she had not required a blood transfusion even after fifty surgical clips had been used to stop the profuse bleeding. After her uterus was removed, it was found to have been torn in many places due to the unborn child's fingernails, for the baby had been a month overdue.

In her anguish, Moi-RA asked Higher Intelligence why she had been brought back to life.

"The answer I received was that I was supposed to do something for the world before I left it for good. I replied that I was ready."

While she was recovering from the surgery, Moi-RA had a vision while she was sitting under a bridge, watching the flow of the water.

"Suddenly, I felt the presence of a great being who put his hand on my crown chakra and whispered with a gentle, soothing voice, *'Do not worry, my child, we will always be with you.'*

"My head was bowed, looking at his feet, feeling the wonderful energy protectively enveloping my whole being. I was so much in awe of his greatness that I dared not look at his face. To see his feet was enough for my soul.

"I felt the blessedness of the healing energy that I was supposed to transmit to humanity.

"This vision guided my life from that moment onward. It led me to the United States. It showed me that I would later meet someone who would do the mission with me."

Moi-RA came to the United States in 1977 after she had taught philosophy and psychology at the University of the City of Manila for ten years. She planned to teach at University of California in Berkeley and complete her doctoral dissertation there. She had told her children that they would return to the Philippines after five years on American soil.

As fate would have it, by 1981, her first husband had passed away and her children had all found themselves suitable mates.

Moi-RA now devoted herself to her duties as a president of a Theosophical Lodge, and she had begun to content herself that such was to be her mission in her present lifetime. Although she had been given a number of readings by clairvoyants that predicted her remarrying, Moi-RA firmly stated that she would never again marry.

But then came the day when she met RA-Ja—and her protestations of remaining single faded away into nothingness.

"When I first met RA-Ja and peered deeply into his light-filled blue eyes, I knew he was the other pea in the pod. I knew that we had finally come together and that we would now be ready for anything. My energy—the energy—was complete. RA-Ja is the most loving being that I have ever known."

RA-Ja said that although it had occurred nearly twenty years ago, he could remember the day well. He had just completed a workshop on Naturopathic Health Principles when a kind lady in the audience came forward to present him with a book entitled *Revelation: The Divine Fire* by Brad Steiger.

"You are one of the men and women that this book is about," she told him. "While you were lecturing, I could see angels and star ships around you."

As RA-Ja examined the book, he received a jolt of spiritual recognition. He had been told in his visions and meditations that one day the Arch-Angels would guide him in es-

tablishing a Spiritual Angel Garden and that
they would build a new Earth from that garden.

"This was the first time I had ever seen in
print accounts of others doing similar kinds
of things. The entire book was filled with
angelic and extraterrestrial lore. Somehow, I
heard a little voice say that this marked a
point in the evolution of Earth. And soon
after that, my angel guides told me that it
was time for a graduation for me. I was to
begin a new leg of my mission on Earth."

After working for over a decade as a
naturopathic physician, teaching in medical
universities and hospitals, working with medical doctors, chiropractors, and having maintained his own clinics in remote and exotic
spa centers of the globe, RA-Ja Dove was now
led by his guides to give up his naturopathic
work and head for Oaxaca and the Yucatan.

He was staying at an ashram when he had
an out-of-body experience in which the Holy
One revealed to him that he must journey to
Palenque's ancient ceremonial site and visit
the Temple of Inscriptions.

RA-Ja donated all of his medical equipment to the ashram. He also gave away his
automobile and bought a bicycle. He would
undertake the long journey to the central
American jungles as a wandering holy man,

taking nothing with him beyond his immediate necessities.

Trusting completely in the angels to protect him, RA-Ja embarked on the pilgrimage that took him to the interior of Mexico, all the way down to Oaxaca, Yucatan, taking time to visit numerous Mayan temples and pyramids.

While in Oaxaca, at Monte Alban in tomb number seven, he experienced another remarkable out-of-body experience in which he seemed to see himself attired in a pharaoh's headdress. He saw himself working with the priests of the One God to establish peace on the land and goodness for the people.

Later, in Tulum, a beautiful ancient Mayan temple complex, RA-Ja joined a group that had gathered one evening to list to the prophecies of a reputable local seeress.

"The seeress explained that I would go back to the United States and meet my twin flame," RA-Ja said. "She said that the woman had been with me in previous lifetimes and that we would find completion in the Aquarian cycle.

"No," I said. "I have been married, and I am not interested in bonding at this time. I believe that I have been called by God to do my spiritual work alone.

" 'Nonetheless,' explained the seeress. 'What I see, will be.' "

* * *

Upon his return to the United States, RA-Ja became severely ill.

"My skin became yellow like parchment paper. I knew that I must have yellow jaundice— or worse, hepatitis.

"After two weeks of suffering, I decided to seek medical assistance, and I received the official diagnosis of a severe case of hepatitis. No cure was known, so it was up to my body's defenses. If it could withstand the disease, I would recover. If not, the end was near!"

RA-Ja visited native elder healers and herbalists and put his own knowledge to work to heal himself. But to no avail.

"I felt that the forces of evil were trying to put a stop to the great mission that had been handed to me. They sought to put a halt to it before I had really been able to get it off the ground.

"I wondered how my Angelic Order could assign me a mission and invest so much into my training, just to let it fail before it began.

"I knew some stories of how some great missions had been subverted by the evil forces— yet somehow I felt a deep sense of winning within me. I knew that I would not fail, but at the same time I didn't know how

I would win. I knew that the Holy Spirit was the only force left that could heal me."

According to RA-Ja the miracle occurred when he was on a bus in Tucson, Arizona, reading *Gods of Aquarius: UFOs and The Transformation of Man* by Brad Steiger. Chapter Eight, "Healing with UFO Energy" told of a man in Denmark who had been cured of a severe case of hepatitis by the low overflight of a UFO.

"This was it! I knew that my Angelic Order was having me read a story exactly like my own, because they wanted to help me. I looked up at the sky and said, 'Isn't it true, my beloved ones? You are having me read these words because you wish to cure me of my disease?' And they whispered ever so softly, *Yes, it is true!*'"

And then, according to RA-Ja, it happened.

"I was healed instantly. I could feel a new surge of energy enter my being. I knew that as I got off the bus, I would be able to walk wherever I wished without getting tired."

Within days, RA-Ja received a message from the Space Brothers that since he was now totally healed, he was to travel to Sounion, Greece, the Temple of Poseidon, for the next stage of his Earth mission.

* * *

While RA-Ja focused and meditated at a secluded beach in Greece, he was surprised when Buddha appeared to him in a very vivid vision. The Buddha told him that he was going to assist his mission by giving him something special. The Buddha further guided RA-Ja to take up a temporary job as a naturopathic physician, nutrition consultant, and a psychiatric counselor.

And then he was back in the United States, hoping that he might find open and receptive minds for the information that he knew it was his mission to share. He felt strongly that the lodges of the Theosophists would present him with a solid network across the country; but he discovered that while the Theosophical Society may have been the harbinger of the New Way at the turn of the century, it seemed to have crystalized its teaching and become resistant to innovative discussions.

But one of their members was listening. And in terms of RA-Ja's mission, she was the most important.

"There she was, an elected Federation President of several Theosophical Lodges. My sweety-hearty, the pink rose of the Philippines, the wise and varicolored lustrous pearl of the Orient, Swami Moi-RA."

RA-Ja realized then why the Buddha had appeared to him in Greece.

"He was bringing me to one of his own kin, an Oriental lady, who certainly lived his core principles. All at once I realized that the seeress in Tulum had been correct. I would be able to work together with this woman. When Buddha said that he was going to help the mission, he had meant that he was bringing my lovely Moi-RA to me. He was adding the other half that would allow the mission to go forth publicly.

"We immediately became co-founders of The Aquarian Perspectives Interplanetary Mission, and we began spreading the word in April of 1985— one year after the impetus for commencing the earth-based portion of the mission was issued in Palenque."

Their wedding ceremony took place on Mount Shasta on April 6, 1985.

"Ah, yes," RA-Ja reflected. "Love beckoned and I responded immediately and without hesitation. We stayed on a honeymoon for three years; and to this day we are as happy as we were twelve hundred billion years ago— when we were created together, male and female, as one."

The Doves' angel guides told them that it was necessary for them to travel around the world, as Jesus did, to see the suffering of the world and the plight of the masses on planet Earth.

They have now pilgrimaged completely around the world, stopping at every major spiritual place and power vortex on the planet.

One of the most common questions the Doves are asked is, "How do you know when you meet your Twin Flame?"

"Once the soul has attained the Grand Union," the Doves answer, "it never forgets. It may take many lesser romances before the Grand Union takes place. But these lesser affairs are but karmic episodes on Love's Grand Path. Every true romance, not infatuation or lust, is the tuning fork of the Twin Flames. There may be a dozen soul mates, but only one Twin Flame!

"When your Twin Flame enters your life, biological age matters not; neither race, color, creed, or cultural origin can keep the inevitable marriage from occurring. The angel seed recognizes and responds."

In Angel Love, as differentiated from earthly love, only the eyes reveal the secret.

"Angel Love is sired from the Soul," state the Doves. "Sex finds its manifestation last. Infatuation or lust are physical and transitory, and they bind those who so indulge to the lower rungs of the spiritual ladder.

"When you have found true love, be ready to give up all and follow your heart's call—for Love speaks but once!

"The love that I feel for RA-Ja is a limitless, unselfish love," Moi-RA said. "It is a love that soars through emotions and thoughts, unharmed, unhindered, ever-flowing, joyfully giving, forward-looking, never-ending, ever-present, not expecting anything in return.

"My love for him is never an addiction, for I give him freedom to be himself, to go at his own pace, to manifest his angelhood. I see the beauty of his soul, the focus of commitment, and the courage of action every moment of the day.

"I feel that I am always with him wherever we are. One thing I notice is the difference in energy when we are apart. It is not complete. But there need not be any sadness, only a lull in inspiration.

"There are not enough words to define my love for RA-Ja; yet I truly believe that if I can show the world that *unconditional love* is possible, then this fallen planet can be redeemed in its full glory. This, I believe, is my true mission: *To live Love!"*

Afterword

One basic lesson that I hope you have received from reading this book is that when you give unconditional angelic love, its energy can never be depleted— for you will also receive it anew from the Angels of Love in a higher dimension. You can never receive imbalance, hatred, envy, or jealousy when you are filled with angelic love. You can never be touched by negative vibrations when you are filled with the energy of the Angels of Love.

Neither can you fill yourself with such love and hold it within your being. You must pour it out upon the world or it will stagnate.

If you bottle up love within you, you will find that it simply cannot keep. It will soon sour. Love must be given so that you may receive it afresh.

Even now as you read these words, feel unconditional, nonjudgmental, angelic love pouring into your body, mind, and spirit.

Feel this angelic love entering your Crown Chakra and filling up your entire physical vessel.

Be aware of it filling your feet, your ankles, your legs, your hips, your stomach, chest, and back. Feel it entering your arms. Sense it moving up your spine. Know that it has entered your neck, your shoulders, your head.

Understand that you are now filled to the crown of your head.

Be aware that you are vibrating, glowing with unconditional love.

Now visualize that there is a golden pyramid above your head, directly over your Crown Chakra.

Understand that this pyramid collects vibrations of love from the angels, then channels it directly into your Crown Chakra. Be aware with all your essence that you have now banished negativity and that your psyche and your physical body are now balanced.

Visualize someone whom you love. See a golden beam of angelic love and light from your Heart Chakra streaking across space and touching that loved one at his or her Heart Chakra. Feel strongly the link-up between the two of you.

Now imagine that you are sending the angelic love and light that the two of you have shared around the world. Visualize that you will touch all those men and women who are depressed, who are feeling unloved, who are feeling imbalanced. See all those who are imprisoned by negativity being able to reach out and make contact with the beautiful energy of angelic love that you are transmitting around the planet.

Feel yourself pouring out unconditional, angelic love and light from your Heart Chakra.

See it streaming all over the Earth.

Know that it is touching the lonely, the despondent, the bitter, the angry, the negative.

Know that it is uplifting their spirits.

Know that it is helping to raise their consciousness.

Know that it is balancing their energies.

Be aware that you are giving and receiving anew the unconditional love vibrations from the Angels of Love. Feel the energy, the strength, the angelic-vibration within the love frequency. Know that the more love that you pour forth from your Heart Chakra, the more love you will receive from the Angels of Love through your Crown Chakra. The more angelic love you transmit, the more you will be energized by the Angels of Love.

Practice this broadcasting of the angelic love vibration on a regular basis, and no negativity can ever pervade your physical being, can ever harm your mind, can ever injure your soul. If you truly fill yourself with unconditional love from the Angels of Love, negativity will never again be able to touch your life.

Give and receive love, and you will immediately become a positive conduit for the Angels of Love, sharing in unparalleled glory and awesome power.

Sixteen

Their Love Was Meant to Be

Lois East told me that she was certain that she and her husband Clay were "truly brought together by the Angels." Lois is a fine artist, who, since 1963, has had the honor of seeing her paintings and sculpture featured in numerous books and national art magazines.

Regarding her unique work with the Angels of Love, she explained that she enters a meditative state, then focuses upon the vibrations of the subject's own angel and renders an interpretation of them in pastels and oils.

Lois and her husband met in 1977 while visiting a meditation class being given by Paul Solomon. Clay said he would not normally have enrolled in the class, since it meant driving diagonally completely across Denver every night for a week. But he felt a strong urging that he take the class. There were no doubts about it. Lois was brought to the class one night as a guest by a friend of hers.

Later, they were told in a reading by Louis Gitner of the Louis Foundation that they had been together many lives before and that they had special work to do. They then realized that angelic influences must have brought them together, working through intuition and through a friend of Lois.

"In the beginning, we were friends, and we spent time together in metaphysical and spiritual classes and various groups. Through these classes and the books we read, our awareness was opened to the Angels and to the truths beyond the physical realm. As our spiritual unfolding grew, we began to see with ever-increasing clarity how our lives were gently guided by the angelic realm."

Lois had moved to the area west of Denver, Colorado, in 1960, and she gained a fine reputation for her paintings of Western landscapes and Native-American life. An art major in college and a former teacher of fine art, she was soon motivated to capture the Angels of Love on her canvas and paper. In 1976, she began studying metaphysics in classes taught by Rev. Allen Miller, and she learned to unfold spiritually.

"In meditation focus, I am able to bring through images and messages from the angels and master teachers for people all over the world who write to me at our post office box number with their birth data and questions. I always say a prayer when I begin, and ask to be a clear channel for the Angels of Light. The paintings of these angels are sent in a heavy mailing tube, and the messages are mailed on tape."

"Clay is very supportive of these endeavors, and many times he reads the questions to me as I am bringing through the messages and the answers. He is a very special and caring partner. It is wonderful to be able to do this work together and to reach out and help others through the paintings and the messages."

Clay is a native of Colorado, a retired engineer, who had hosted a study group of the Manly P. Hall books in his home for many years prior to his meeting Lois.

"In the early 1980s, Clay and I were told that we would be freer in our lives in many areas in the years to come. His first wife had multiple sclerosis for many years, before she passed away; and I had been married for more than twenty years to an architect. When we met, I was concentrating on my fine art career of painting people and landscapes. Although Clay had studied many of the ancient metaphysical teachings, my previous spiritual work had pretty much been limited to having taught Sunday School when my two children, Tara and Craig, were young. I had also illustrated childrens' Bible books."

Lois and Clay were married in December, 1983.

"We feel that marriage in the highest sense is not only gazing into each other's eyes, but also in gazing together in the same direction.

"And we are very blessed by being in conscious communication with the angels. In meditation, I bring through messages from my spiritual helpers, Ra and Sha-Lin, as well as words from individuals' angels."

In her paintings, Lois most often depicts the angels in colors of light lavender, gold, pink, peach, white, light blue, and magenta.

"These are all light and beautiful colors that join the abstract lightness of watercolors and pastels with the hazy translucency of the angelic forms. I fashion paintings that bring forth that which I see in meditation and prayer—the Light dimensions.

"When we meditate," Lois said, "we are focused into the Light. We are never alone."

Lois and Clay have plans to reproduce many of the angelic images which she has received on prints and greeting cards.

"I feel that I have been given this talent by God, and I have chosen this direction in my career with the help of the angels. It is now time to share these angelic images with thousands of people who also love the angels."

According to Lois, an angelic entity named Aranaea told her that within the Angelic realm, beautiful entities express the greatest love in the Angelic Kingdom of Light. The activities of these honored beings never cease.

They are attracted to the seeking many.

They see the need; they feel the thoughts; they shower love; they envision the perfection within the human embodiment.

Therefore, as you know, the mind is the builder. Many choices are within the minds of many who are seeking health of the body.

It is beneficial to seek the Angels. They want only to shower healing, to teach and to share love.

They want only to love.

Seventeen

Patience and Faith

Fay Marvin Clark of Perry, Iowa, was a highly valued mentor of mine during my formative years as an author and researcher in the mid-1960s. Although I had been exploring the unknown ever since I was a child and had begun publishing when I was fifteen, it was reassuring to me to meet a wise and cheerful silver-haired gentleman, who had begun his own paranormal explorations before I had been born. And it only enhanced our friendship that in those days, Fay was a dead ringer for Claude Rains, an actor that I had very much admired as a youth.

When Fay passed away on October 23, 1991, he was married to Marvel, a charming lady whom I had met many years before they had become man and wife. I knew intuitively that she and Fay had been guided to be as one by the Angels of Love, and I knew that their relationship of many years had undergone numerous transitions that must have required patience, unconditional love, and genuine acts of caring.

"I miss Fay so much," Marvel told me, "but I have many indications of his presence and his continued love. I love him more than any person I have ever known, and I am sure that our angelic guides or some higher power helped to arrange our meeting in this lifetime."

Marvel said that their meeting had not occurred at the best of timing for either of them, for they were each married to another at the time. Of less consequence was their difference in age. She was thirty-one; he was fifty-six.

"But just knowing each other was wonderful—and when we finally did get our eleven wonderful years together, it was like Heaven on Earth for both of us. I *know* that Fay and I were destined to meet."

Through a somewhat extended process, Marvel had become aware of Fay's Hiawatha Publishing Company in Hiawatha, Iowa, and she learned that he had been involved in metaphysical research for many years with his first wife, Adeline.

Marvel herself had pursued her own psychic and spiritual studies in Perry, Iowa, since about 1954.

"I had discovered the Edgar Cayce readings, and I had communicated with the Association for Research and Enlightenment (A.R.E.) at Virginia Beach, Virginia. By such correspondence, I had placed my name on their mailing list, and since Fay was on the Board of Trustees for the A.R.E., he was able to acquire use of the list. Although he only used that mailing list for one six-month period sometime in 1962, I received a catalog from his Hiawatha Book Store. I placed the catalog in a drawer, and I didn't run across it again for a year or so."

When the catalog resurfaced, Marvel glanced at the list of books and made a mental note to herself to one day drive to Hiawatha and visit the book store.

And then *something* or *someone* caused her to sit down and dash off a quick note, asking what hours it would be possible to visit the Hiawatha Book Store.

"In three days I had a nice reply from Fay, saying that he *knew* from my letter that I was someone that he very much wanted to meet."

After a series of short correspondences that continued back and forth for many weeks, Marvel finally walked into the Hiawatha Book Store on August 16, 1963.

"That meeting was to change my life forever.

"Fay had a showcase of beautiful gemstones just inside his door, and we spent the first two hours looking at and talking about the various stones. All my life I have loved gemstones, and I had studied a lot about them. I even had a good-sized collection of my own."

As they were engrossed in an examination of the various attractive and fascinating stones, Fay paused in his conversation, looked deep into Marvel's eyes, and said: "This has not been the first time that we have met. I have known you before— many times."

Then he went right on with his explanation of a particular stone before Marvel had a chance to say anything in response and as if he had said nothing at all out of the ordinary.

"Of course I wouldn't have known what to say anyway. Later, as I came to know Fay,, I knew that he would *never* say *anything* like that to *anyone*— even if he *did* have such thoughts.

"I am still certain to this day that those words came out spontaneously— as though he had no control over what he had said.

"Many months later, we talked briefly about the incident. He agreed that he would not under normal circumstances have said such a thing to anyone, but he did remember having said those words to me; and he went on to say that when I had first walked in the door to the store, he had the most powerful sense of *knowing* me.

"On the way home that evening of August 16, 1963, all I could remember were Fay's eyes. I seemed to know them, and a deep bond of love was there instantly. From that day on, Fay was the 'Light of my life.' "

Marvel was married at the time with two little daughters.

"I was very busy and involved with my family, my music career, and my spiritual studies. I had no intention then of obtaining a divorce. Such thoughts never entered my mind.

"Then, early in 1968, my husband left me and my little girls. We divorced several months later."

It was not until the fall of 1968 while she was working for Fay at his publishing company in Perry, Iowa, that the two of them finally shared the deep love that they had felt for one another since their first meeting five years earlier.

"We were on cloud nine, but there were other responsibilities, and it was not the right time for us to be together— and it would be twelve more years before the 'right timing' came for us."

Adeline had passed away in 1961; and in 1965, Fay married Mary Luther, a close friend of Marvel's.

"In fact, they had even met at my home when I hosted a metaphysical meeting."

Mary passed away in May of 1979, and Fay and Marvel were married on September 6, 1980.

"We had eleven wonderful years together until his death from a heart attack in October of 1991. Each day reconfirmed the deep love and caring that we felt for each other.

"Fay was twenty-five years older than I, but this made no difference in the joy we had in sharing our lives over the thirty years that we knew each other.

"I am certain that our love continues on the other side. Love is forever!"

Eighteen

Beautiful Tapestry
of the Spirit

For many years now, John Harricharan, the award-winning author of *When You Can Walk on Water, Take the Boat* and *Morning Has Been All Night Coming*, has been one of my closest friends. Since I knew that John and his lovely wife Mardai had been brought together by the Angels of Love, I asked him to share the touching story of their loving relationship for the readers of this book.

John's forefathers had traveled from India to work on the farms of British Guiana, the only British Colony on the northern coast of South America. In the small fishing and farming village where he was born, Muslims, Hindus, and Christian converts lived together in peace and relative prosperity.

His parents were Hindus, but the Harricharans had many Muslim and Christian friends. The people of various religious faiths cooperated with one another and tolerated the multitude of beliefs that had become normal in such a diverse society. During religious holidays, the villagers would all visit the different churches, noting more similarities than differences in beliefs.

"About the age of eleven," John told me, "I started attending the Christian churches, as well as our own Hindu temple. Later on, I became a Christian; and my father, a liberal Hindu, encouraged my church-going and even attended with me on a number of occasions. At the same time, I still visited the Hindu temple."

John was baptized and confirmed into the Lutheran denomination of Christianity.

Village life revolved around sowing and reaping, between the dry season and the wet season. And in the evenings, the younger boys would listen to the elders tell stories of their youth.

"We would sit by a wood fire, the flames

fanned by the trade winds of the Atlantic, totally entranced by the tales of guardian angels, friendly ghosts, and unseen influences that had made their presence felt. I grew up believing, as Shakespeare's Hamlet did, that 'There are more things in heaven and earth, Horatio, than are dreamt of in your philosophy.' "

High school was not mandatory. It was an honor. And some of the village children were fortunate enough to attend high school in the city while the others went to work on the farms with friends and relatives.

John's father had been unable to finish fourth grade when he was a boy, but later in life, he believed so strongly that he should educate his children that John was one of the fortunate ones to attend high school.

"I have always felt a guiding hand in my affairs in life. Even my earliest memories reflected a wonderful world of friendly beings who were willing to help me. It was as if an angel sat on my shoulder and whispered to me when I wasn't sure which way to go or what to do."

It was during his second year in high school that an incident occurred which was to have a major effect on John's entire life.

"To attend high school in those days, one had to pay certain tuition fees. Because of some financial problems in the family, my fees were not paid in time; and I was asked to leave school.

"When I returned home and told my dad what had happened, I could see the sadness in his eyes and hear it in his voice. He had worked very hard to earn the money for my school fees— and now there was confusion."

John's father, a simple farmer from the village, always seemed to listen to an inner voice. After a moment of quiet, he looked at his son and said, "There is a man of importance who lives in the city, not too far from where your school is.

"I hear that he is very kind and that he helps many people. He is also a pastor of a Lutheran church, and so may be inclined to help us— especially since you attend services every week. We will talk to him about our problem, and then we'll see what else to do."

Early the next morning, John and his father set out on the long trip to the city.

"We caught the bus at 5:30 A.M.," John remembered. "We reached the ferry at 7:00, and finally arrived in the city at 9:00 A.M. We asked directions, and we eventually arrived at the home of the Lutheran pastor."

John was only twelve or thirteen, but he

recalled vividly the sense of excitement as if something extraordinary were about to happen.

His father rang the doorbell. John would tell that he was nervous and worried.

What if this man couldn't— or wouldn't— help them? What if they were forced to return to the village without any hope?

If that were so, John would never be able to finish high school, and all of his days would be spent working in the village fields as his father was doing— and as his father before him had done.

Such thoughts were crossing John's mind when the door opened and a maid, dressed in a white uniform, asked their business.

"We are here to speak to the master of the house," John's father said solemnly. "We would be most grateful for a few moments of his time."

"Do you have an appointment?" the maid asked haughtily.

"My son and I . . . we did not realize that an appointment was necessary."

"The master is very busy. You'll have to make an appointment and return another day. He just can't see everyone who turns up on his doorstep."

John's heart fell as he heard those ominous words of dismissal.

His father, however, held his head high and told the imperious maid that they would wait until her master could see them.

Before the maid could say another word, John remembered, they heard footsteps, and a regal-looking man came through the door. The maid held the door open for him as he looked at the father and son with kindly, but questioning, eyes.

"I was just leaving," the pastor said, "but I do have a few moments. What can I do for you?"

John's father, sensing that time was precious, did not hesitate. "We need your help, sir."

"Come with me, then. Let's sit in my office, and you can tell me what you need."

The two nervous villagers followed the pastor up the stairs and into his office. He motioned for them to sit while he sat behind a giant desk that occupied one corner of the room.

After John's father had introduced them, he quickly explained why they had come into the city to see him.

The pastor listened intently and took some notes. After he had asked a few questions, he smiled and told them to go home.

"Don't worry anymore about this," he advised them with calm assurance. "I know the principal of the school. I will take care of this whole business of fees. I'll also make sure that it never happens again . . ."

The pastor was unable to finish his sentence, because at that moment there was a loud bang on the door.

The door flew open as a little girl, pedaling furiously on a tricycle, rushed into the pastor's office. She could not have been more than five or six years old.

The pastor smiled and said, "That's my daughter, Mardai."

The girl turned and headed out the door, running over John's foot with her tricycle in the process.

She turned around, smiled up at John. "Sorry."

And then she was gone.

"As I stood there," John recalled, "a strange, sweet sadness came over— and a still, small voice whispered in my ear: *'You'll marry her one day.'*

"I quickly regained my composure as my dad thanked the good man for his help before we left his home.

"But that was how I met Mardai, the one who, years later, was to become my wife. It was as if my guardian angel had orchestrated the entire affair so that I could get a preview of coming events. She was only six, and I was thirteen when this initial meeting occurred."

The problems at high school were solved, just as the Lutheran pastor had promised. The years went by, and every once in a while, John would recall the time when his father and he had visited the kind pastor in the city. It appeared unlikely that he would ever see the clergyman and his daughter again. They were from the city, and they socialized with the highest levels of society— while John was from a small country village of fishermen and farmers.

But, as John phrases it, "The angels of God looked down on this country boy and smiled!"

John graduated from high school, and the world seemed to be full of opportunities.

Word came to the village that the church at the outskirts of town would be expanded and that a very famous pastor would temporarily stay in the parsonage until the expansion plans would be accomplished. John was surprised when he found out that the new pastor was the same one whom his dad and he had visited years earlier.

"I discreetly inquired as to whether his family would stay there with him. I was disappointed when I was told that they would visit only on weekends. I was also informed that he had only one child, the daughter whom I had first seen on the tricycle."

The day finally came when John saw Mardai again.

"This time she was not a little girl, but a young lady with all her hopes and dreams shining brightly. Again, that strange otherworldly feeling came over me as I looked at her. Again, the voice whispered in my heart and soul, *'She is the one you'll marry. She will be your wife and help you do the things that you came here to do.'*

"The angels seemed to have a way with words. It seemed so ridiculous—and yet, there was a ring of truth to it."

The time came for John to leave the shores of that little colony on the northern coast of South America to further his education. With the help of Mardai's father, he was able to enter a university in the United States with a full scholarship.

"University life was very different from life in the little village. In time, I graduated with honors and went on to graduate school.

"I had my share of girlfriends, but all through the years, I would think of Mardai.

I wrote poems about her, and I dreamed about seeing her again."

One day, years later, John received a letter from Mardai's father. The family had relocated to Canada to begin a new life after leaving behind all the political problems and the near civil war that had shaken Guiana. The pastor told John that they would be spending the summer with relatives in New York City and that he would like John to visit them and to have dinner with them as soon as it would be possible for him to do so.

"The threads of time weave strange patterns in the fabric of life, and so it was, through strange coincidences and synchronicities, I found myself in New York City. By this time, I had begun working for a Fortune 500 company, and my future seemed bright. All I can say is that the Angels of Love and Mercy had smiled upon me again!"

Not long after John had reunited with Mardai and her family in New York City, they moved to a small town in Pennsylvania. As destiny would dictate the scenario, John soon relocated from the city to a small town across the river in New Jersey. In such close proximity, he would visit Mardai and her family every once in a while. And the more he stopped by, the better friends he became with Mardai.

"Some things seemed to be destined. They make no sense if we try to reason them out. If we do attempt to unravel their mystery, we only serve to confuse ourselves even further.

"Thus it was that Mardai and I were brought together across oceans and countries and time. No longer the little girl, she had grown into a beautiful, charming young woman.

"The words of the Angel of Love were finally fulfilled. Mardai and I became engaged; and a year later, we were married. She was only nineteen, and I was all of twenty-six. Our marriage was one of those special unions that only seemed to have been made possible with the help of other dimensional friends. A few years later, our first child, Malika, was adopted, followed by her brother, Jonathan, four years later."

Mardai encouraged John to write and to publish his award-winning allegorical work, *When You Can Walk on Water, Take the Boat,* a book which creatively portrays the subtle interaction of other dimensional beings in the flow of human experience.

"She always believed in me—even when I

didn't believe in myself. Sometimes I thought
that she wasn't brought to me by an angel of
love, but that she herself *was* an Angel of
Love."

Mardai and John spent many happy years
together. She stayed by his side through all
his trials and tribulations, never complaining,
always encouraging, and always having a kind
word for others.

But the Angels of Love had not told John
what the rest of the story would be like.

"One day, unexpectedly, Mardai was diagnosed with cancer. She fought a valiant bat-
tle, but she finally left the Earth plane to
continue her angelic work on other, perhaps
brighter, shores.

"It's been a few years since she has been
gone, but sometimes it feels like yesterday. I
often wish that I could share my thoughts
with her.

"On quiet evenings, I sit on my back porch
in our home in Marietta, Georgia, feeling the
wind blow through my hair. I look up to the
skies and see the twinkling stars far, far away.
If I let my mind wander, I can almost hear
Mardai singing a song of joy and love as she
used to do years ago.

"Perhaps, once upon a time, there walked

on Earth an Angel of Love named Mardai. Perhaps she had intended to stay with me for only a little while before she went back to join her other angel friends. And yet I cannot help feeling that the ties that bind us span eternity itself."

Nineteen

The Greatest Lesson
of the Heart

Sometime in the mid-1970s, I made the acquaintance of two healers who had begun to gain a growing national reputation for quietly channeling what they considered to be otherworldly energy to accomplish physical healings. What struck me as delightfully ironic was that Lorraine and Victor Darr conducted their healing ministry in Rochester, Minnesota, the home of the august Mayo Clinic, a mighty bulwark of conventional medicine.

Neither of these two soft-spoken people made any kind of extravagant claims for their ability to channel healing energy, and they expressed amazement whenever folks flew in from California, New Jersey, or one of the Canadian provinces to consult with them. It was apparent to me that this shy, unassuming couple sought only to serve their fellow humans in the best way that they could.

It was on September 2, 1974, that Lorraine began to receive automatic writing— at first from a spirit entity who claimed to be her grandmother, then later from various elevated beings.

Often Lorraine would enter a state of light trance and permit the entities to write through her and channel various instructions, advice, and criticisms that she and Vic might then use in their healing ministry.

Vic and Lorraine treated all manner of ailments, and they began to receive "patients" from as far away as Europe. Some people swore that they were able to see a white-colored energy flow emanate from Vic's hands.

An exceedingly down-to-earth kind of fellow, Vic never spoke of psychic phenomena, mysticism, or his ability to become a co-creator with multidimensional beings. He was appreciative of these Light Beings' assistance in his work, but he really attributed all blessings to self-awareness. When people became totally aware of themselves and their potentialities, he argued, then they automatically became citizens of other dimensions of being.

Vic had also heeded the Master Healer's admonition, "Physician, heal thyself." He was a former steelworker who had been injured in a factory and had been left partially paralyzed. By that time, he was already active in his healing ministry, and while he lay in a hospital bed, people came from miles around to receive healings from him.

The irony of the entire situation struck him with powerful impact one night. He spent two and one-half hours working on himself, during which time he admits that he sweated a great deal. Within a day and a half, he walked out of the hospital.

He had also once worn a hearing aid and had been told by doctors that his damaged sense of hearing was beyond help. Again, by working on himself, Vic was able to discard his hearing aid.

I stayed in touch with the Darrs throughout the years. Victor made his transition to the Great Mystery in 1993; but now, twenty years after our first meeting, I have asked Lorraine to describe the lifetime in which these two light workers lived under the guidance of angelic spirit beings.

* * *

The tale began, Lorraine said in answer to my query, on a summer's day with a group of young women gathered together in a dormitory room on the campus of what was then known as Teachers College of Iowa during the 1949 summer session.

"None of us had teaching jobs for fall, so we opened the Sunday paper to the want ads. My way of scanning and assessing ads was quite different from my friends'. I held a pencil raised above the paper and moved it in a spiral toward the listings saying, 'Where the pencil lands, I will apply for a position.'

"I was accepted to teach third and fourth grade at Hartford, Iowa, a small town twenty miles southeast of Des Moines, and that was where I would begin a life adventure of more than forty years. That was where Victor Darr lived— the person the angels were guiding me to meet."

Victor had served as a military policeman in Japan during the early days of the occupation, and he had lived in Hartford with his family ever since he had been discharged from the army. He had two younger brothers in high school, and his youngest brother was in third grade.

Many times after she had begun her teaching duties, Lorraine asked herself what she was doing there in that little town of two hundred people where nothing seemed to happen.

One Friday night in February, six months after she had arrived in Hartford, she and a friend, the instrumental music teacher, went to the tiny cafe to visit with people from the local community.

Lorraine learned later that someone had dared Vic to ask the "new teacher" to dance. Never one to pass up a dare, he punched in a tune on the juke box and asked her to dance.

"I did not realize then that the universal Powers That Be had accomplished the task of bringing two teachers together to begin an adventure like no other," Lorraine said.

"Vic felt from the start that we were to be together— whereas I took about four weeks to know and to accept that we would be married."

By the time school ended in May, they had rented an apartment. Their marriage took place on June 11, 1950.

"Basically, our married life unfolded in eleven-year cycles. The first eleven in and around Hartford, where our five children began their schooling. The second eleven commenced in 1961 when Spirit pushed us to move to New Hampton, Iowa, which was my birthplace. Vic joined the crew in a car dealership and auto repair business that my father had built from scratch. This was a difficult move because Vic and the children really didn't want to leave Hartford. I just 'felt' we needed to move.

"But whether the whole family wanted to move or not, the angels had brought us there to undergo some very big changes."

A little more than a week after their move to New Hampton, Lorraine's mother was diagnosed as having a very fast-spreading type of cancer. She died thirteen months after surgery. Lorraine's father passed away in his sleep eighteen months later.

Lorraine taught for another five and a half years, then left public school teaching forever due to ill health.

It was at this time that Vic began studying the healing arts of reflexology and zone therapy in his spare time. He found that both methods, which deal with pressure points on the feet, were great aids to assisting people to heal themselves.

This was also the period of time when Vic hurt his back at work, and the Darrs interpreted his "being released from work by an accident," as a sign that they should now expand their healing work.

In 1972, at the onset of their third eleven-year-cycle, they chose to move to Rochester, Minnesota, ten blocks from the Mayo Clinic, to establish their healing ministry.

"After twenty-three years of living with Vic, he had shared very little with me about his paranormal abilities. I had observed that he always seemed to 'know' what the children were going to do, but he appeared reluctant to reveal too much of his inner self.

"I was not yet fully aware of my own inner abilities, because of all the emotional lessons in which I was so deeply enmeshed.

"So there we were, placed by Spirit in an orthodox healing city, prepared to expand our lives, thoughts, and abilities by working on peoples' feet. I often wonder if the angels and guiding spirits smile or laugh *at* or *with* us Earth humans as we learn and grow.

"Our third eleven-year-cycle— from 1972 to 1983— was by far the most momentous time of change in our journey. Here we were grandparents and starting forth on a new path. We had always been workaholics, so our guides filled us with energy and pushed us along."

After the move to Rochester, Minnesota, Lorraine is convinced that there were many aspects to their newly begun activities which were clearly apparent to all who knew them.

"First, the angels and Spirit broke down Victor's walls and helped him to feel secure enough to use a whole new set of 'tools' to expand his consciousness as much as possible each day. His initial work on the feet became the foundation upon which he built to include body energy balancing, harmonizing physical body systems, and allowing healing energies to flow through his hands, heart, and thoughts."

Victor came to be known as "the man with the magic fingers." Lorraine received channeling that informed them that a medical doctor and a chiropractor in Spirit would work through his hands and guide his thoughts. He accepted their help, and they would often move his hands differently from what he had intended so that he might discover a previously undiscovered aspect of the patient's problem.

Also, in 1974, Lorraine began her work with automatic writing.

"At first I had much fear about such things. Spirit first had a grandmother of mine speak to me and answer questions. It was much less frightening to me to be able to speak to her.

"Then Spirit used many different entities who wrote through me, giving information and teachings.

"After four months of such writing to break down my fears, my guiding spirit added direct voice channeling in which I would speak in voices not my own. This was terrifying to me at first, but I soon grew to accept the phenomenon with greater willingness on my part."

Lorraine also began to practice "journaling" at this time.

"I would write down all of my feelings and emotions regarding this new life. I found this process to be very cleansing, and it helped to bring clarity to my mind. The journaling and the voice channeling were the major links to my Higher Self.

"Spirit gave instructions, information, support, and a great deal of energy for both Victor and myself through my voice and written channeling. Our awareness was growing and expanding at a furious rate."

The paranormal and healing abilities of Vic and Lorraine continued to develop at a very rapid pace during their years in Rochester. Lorraine said that she sometimes felt as though she were on a fast-moving train that made very few stops.

"There were times when I felt as though I had been blind and was just learning how to see. Thankfully, the spirit helpers were always there to help me put the pieces together. I spent a great deal of time in prayer and meditation."

The Darrs remained in Rochester for nearly six years. They traveled and worked in parts of Illinois, Wisconsin, Iowa, and Minnesota, sharing their healing and teaching abilities with individuals and with groups.

"From mid-1979 through 1982, Victor and I were like a mobile healing unit that was sent here and there to encounter new situations and to help people.

"The angels had helped me to learn how to 'read' people's physical body systems. I could read their auras and discover their individual energy systems.

"Neither Vic nor myself had ever had any human teachers to guide us and to direct the explosive manner in which doorways to other worlds had opened for us. All of our steps— both hesitantly and confidently— were taken only with the guidance of our spirit helpers. We had to learn to trust, trust, trust our spirit teachers through all of our earthly learnings."

In November of 1982, Vic and Lorraine moved to Lake Forest, Illinois where Spirit guided them to live with a woman for five to six months. During that time, their host organized a trip to Egypt with the Darrs.

"What we could not know was that that fateful trip to Egypt would close the doors on our working together as a couple and open new vistas for our individual pathways in the future. After thirty-three years together, we would now begin to walk alone."

Lorraine remembered that the act of visiting certain places in Egypt was like "going home." And always for her there was the sense of timelessness.

Angelic beings had given Vic a design that enabled him to create from brass welding rods a work that resembled a flower and which he called a fl°w-er. Their popularity soon placed them in private homes and in metaphysical and healing centers all over the United States. In Egypt, Vic intuitively carried one of the smallest of the pieces into many tombs, temples, and even the king's chamber of the great pyramid.

On their first night in Cairo, Lorraine beheld the great pyramid illuminated with floodlights. Shocked, she uttered, "That's not how we left it!"

She was the only one of the ten people on the tour who was not allowed to crawl up inside the great pyramid to meditate in the king's chamber.

"A large hand on my head turned me out of the line to go back outside," she said. "As I sat on a block near the entrance to the pyramid, I cried and asked why I had not been allowed to experience the chamber like everyone else.

"The answer came immediately: 'You did not come to Egypt to go inside *anything* but *yourself!*'

"That was hard for me to accept, yet I had to comply."

After they returned from Egypt, Lorraine and Vic moved to Spring Green, Wisconsin, and presented Crystal Conferences there and other places. The following year on her birthday, April 3, 1984, they moved to Westby, Wisconsin.

"By June of that year, Vic and I were on our separate pathways, each of us growing enormously toward the attainment of linking the full understandings of Heaven and Earth to become radiant lights. Vic moved to Franklin, North Carolina, in the Smoky Mountains. I stayed on a farm in Westby for five years, then began to spend time between the Midwest and Arizona."

In June of 1990, Victor suffered a stroke and spent two weeks in a coma. After six months in a hospital, he came home to be cared for by his second wife, Nancy.

The angels took a hand again when Nancy asked Lorraine if she could please come to look after Vic for a week while she took a vacation to stave off exhaustion. Lorraine consented to come to North Carolina to take care of her ex-husband.

"After I was back home in Tucson, I spent much time in prayer, listening and learning more of trust. Spirit and the angels kept saying to me, 'You are to take care of Victor!'

"I finally consented— part of me *knowing* it was right to do . . . and part of me saying, 'Why are you doing this? It's crazy!' "

In June of 1991, Victor flew into Des Moines from North Carolina. Lorraine had driven from Tucson to pick him up and to begin a new life together.

"Our new life lasted one year and eight months. We had both changed a great deal— yet the Soul love and personal regard for one another had never changed.

"The divine guidance in our relationship created the space and the time to enjoy each other and to complete the purposeful times on Earth that we had worked together. We released each other on all spiritual levels of interaction. It was good for both of us.

"The actual closing came about two days after I had a heart attack, lying on a hospital bed. On the morning of February 23, 1993, Victor's soul-spirit disconnected the lifeline to his body.

"The essence of Victor was standing by the Earth body when Jesus came to him, asking if he was ready to go.

"Victor said, yes, so in the early light of dawn, he began his next life phase in spirit.

"I was also beginning anew, lying in a hospital bed, agreeing to by-pass surgery, knowing that Spirit would carry me on where I needed to be, all owing, trusting. This is what life is as the love of One lives fully in all hearts."

Lorraine told me that Victor has communicated with her from the other side on a number of occasions.

On July 5, 1994, she received this message from Spirit regarding the Angels of Love:

* * *

"Angels appear to humans in whatever form the receiving human holds in his or her thoughts at the time.

"The greater *Love* of Being is a force that has many forms to use as the situation requires. *Love* denotes Soul-Spirit sense. *Love* is of human sense. *Love* of being is a force we are to learn again to use.

"Angels give us images and thoughts from the knowingness to guide and prepare us each day. They often appear at critical moments to ease our learnings and to leave us 'wondering' and 'knowing.'

"Thank the *Love* of God for Angels!"

Part Four

Angelic Love: Experiencing Its Sweetness and Light

Twenty

Reaffirming a Telepathic Link with Your Beloved

Telepathy as you no doubt understand, simply means that one can, through the mind, make contact with another.

When you first experiment with telepathy, you may find to your surprise that you will soon hear from someone whom you have had in mind a great deal— almost as if the person knew that you wanted to hear from him or her.

If you deliberately set out to "reach" someone by your mental telephone, you may encounter a delay in receiving an actual *physical* response. This should not discourage you, for you will be able to *know* that your telepathic message reached its destination if you felt a *mental* response at the time.

If you are visualizing the recipient of your telepathic message clearly and you suddenly feel a small tingle in your arm or solar plexus, you will *know* that your message has been received on some level of that individual's consciousness. You don't have to imagine this response, for it will be real enough.

Before attempting to make telepathic transfer with your loved one, it is best to sit quietly for a few moments.

Take three comfortably deep breaths. This will give added power to the broadcasting station of your psyche.

Visualize the vastness of space.

Contemplate the meaninglessness of time.

See yourself as a circle that grows and grows until it occupies the Earth, the galaxy.

See yourself blending into a Oneness with the Living God, All-That-Is.

Now visualize the loved one whom you wish to contact. See him (or her . . . use whichever pronoun is appropriate) plainly. Feel his presence.

In your mind, speak to him as if he were

sitting there before you. Do *not* speak to him aloud. Speak to him mentally.

Take three comfortably deep breaths, revving up your broadcasting power.

Mentally relay the message that you wish your loved one to receive from you.

Once you have transmitted the message, ask him to call you or to get somehow in touch with you on the physical level.

RECEIVING IMPRESSIONS OF YOUR LOVER'S TRUE FEELINGS

If your loved one has not yet made the commitment of love that you have been hoping to receive, you may wish to find out telepathically how the loved one in question truly feels about you. Here is how you may make your mind a receiving set for your lover's thoughts and feelings.

Sit quietly and breathe slowly in comfortably deep breaths.

Picture in your mind your loved one sitting or standing there before you. Don't beat around the bush. Get right to the bottom line. Ask him (her) point-blank: *"Do you really love me?"*

If you receive a very warm and gentle impulse or tingle, you will immediately become aware of the fact that the loved one in question really loves you.

If you receive a cool impulse, the loved one may not truly love you and may even be deceitful in dealing with you.

TRANSMITTING HEALING THOUGHTS TO LOVED ONES WHO ARE ILL OR INJURED

It is possible to send healing energy to those loved ones who are ill or injured and who may be separated from you by some distance. You must understand, of course, that it is not you who can heal, but your unselfish act of tuning in to the Infinite Mind of All-That-Is that does so.

The *most vital point* in telepathically healing or helping another is this: You must actually *see* the desired condition and *know* that it will be accomplished.

When you send healing thoughts to your loved one who is ill, you must visualize your loved one as being *completely* healed.

You must *not* permit yourself to visualize him as he is at the present time.

You must *not* see him in the throes of his illness or the misery of his accident.

You must actually see him in *the desired state of health* and in your heart and mind *know* that it will be so.

If you should happen to be concerned about a loved one who has a very bad habit or dependency that needs correcting, you may also send mental pictures to that person of his hating the habit or the dependency so much that he, of his own free choice, will give it up.

When you visualize your loved one who is plagued with the bad habit or dependency, he, too, must be seen as *triumphant* over the problem.

You must visualize him as having *completely forsaken* the habit or dependency.

Only by seeing the habit or dependency as *totally negated* will the problem be discontinued.

If you have learned that a loved one has become bereaved, you may telepathically send him a comforting thought that the Divine Will has been done and that It will soon send solace.

* * *

In all the above instances, always remember the cardinal rule: *You must actually see the desired conditions and know that it will be so.*

Twenty-one

Manifesting a Vision
of Love

In order to achieve the utmost success with this exercise, be certain to place yourself in a very restful, meditative state. It would be very helpful to play some romantic classical or New Age music in the background. Just be certain that whatever musical accompaniment you select does not contain any lyrics to distract you.

You may study the following procedure so that you can retain the essence of its steps in order to guide yourself to the vision. Or you may prerecord your voice, giving yourself step-by-step instructions from your cassette recorder.

Once you have attained a comfortable state of relaxation, proceed on the path to attain your vision of love:

Visualize yourself surrounded by a violet light. Feel the warmth of the light from the Angels of Love beginning to stimulate your Crown Chakra.

Become one with the feeling of being loved unconditionally by the Angels of Love—beings of light who have always loved you. Sense the presence of an angelic intelligence that you have always known was near to you ever since you were a child.

Be aware of a sensation of warmth in both your Heart Chakra and your Crown Chakra.

Be aware of a ray of light connecting your individual spirit essence to the higher vibration of the Angels of Love.

Visualize that the violet light has now acquired a tinge of pink. See it begin to swirl around you, moving faster and faster until it begins to acquire a form and a substance.

Visualize now the shape of a body . . . hair . . . a beautiful smile on a loving face.

Become especially aware of the eyes.

Feel the love, the unconditional love, that flows out to you from those beautiful eyes.

You have an inner knowing that your guide

has come to take you to a special dimension where you will be able to receive a clear image of the one who will be *your life partner!*

You will be able to receive a clear image of the one who will be your partner in love. (If you are already with your life partner, substitute the command: *You will be able to receive a clearer understanding of the true nature of your love relationship. You will be able to comprehend a clearer understanding of your connection to the Angels of Love.)*

Whatever it is that you most need to know about your love relationship for your fullest good and gaining will be revealed to you in this holy place.

Your angel guide stretches forth a loving hand. Take that hand in your own.

Feel angelic love flowing through you. Feel the vibration of an angelic being who has always loved you.

Feel the vibration of love from one who has loved you with pure, heavenly, unconditional love.

Feel the vibration of love from one who has come to take you to a special place where a *profound vision of love awaits you!*

See a violet mist clouding up around you

as you begin to move through time and space with your angelic guide.

Feel yourself moving through time and space.

At the count of five, you will be in the holy dimension of angelic love. One . . . two . . . three . . . four . . . five!

See yourself now in this holy dimension of love and light.

You may be seeing yourself in a beautiful garden that lies before a majestic temple.

You may be seeing yourself in a magical place in a lovely forest.

You may be seeing yourself high in some mountain retreat.

There is now a vibration in the air as if bells are chiming.

At that sound, that signal, a wise teacher comes to meet you. *(The teacher may be either male or female in form, whichever you prefer.)*

Look deeply into the eyes of the beloved teacher.

Become totally aware of this teacher. See the teacher's clothes . . . body . . . face . . . mouth . . .

Your angelic guide has once again materialized beside you, and you are walking together behind the teacher.

You are now walking in a tunnel. The teacher is taking you to a secret place.

Experience your emotions as you walk silently between your angel guide and your spirit teacher. Feel deeply your expectations.

Be keenly aware of any aromas . . . sounds . . . sights.

Now you are in a great room.

Look around you slowly.

See statues . . . paintings . . . works of art arranged around the secret room. Each object has been designed to honor the mission of the Angels of Love.

Now the teacher is showing you a great crystal that is supported on a golden tripod.

The teacher says that the great crystal is a powerful transmitter for the Angels of Love.

When you are permitted to lean forward and gaze into the crystal, you will be allowed to see the vision of love for which you have come to this holy dimension of awareness and unconditional love.

The teacher says that you will only see that which is meant for you to see for your utmost good and gaining.

You will see only what is necessary for you to see for your present level of understanding.

You will see a beautiful vision of love that will be completely individualized for you and for your particular needs at this moment in your spiritual evolution.

Your teacher tells you to get ready. Prepare yourself mentally for your vision.

Step forward to the crystal.

Lean forward . . . and see your vision of love *now!*

(*Allow three or four minutes for the vision to manifest.*)

Now with the beautiful images of the glorious vision of love clearly fixed in your memory, return to full wakefulness at the count of five. At the count of five, you will awaken feeling better than you have in weeks and weeks, in months and months. You will feel positive energy in body, mind, and spirit— and you will be filled with unconditional love from the Angels of Love.

One . . . coming awake. Two, more and more awake. Three, opening your eyes. Four, waking up and feeling wonderful. *Five* . . . wide awake and feeling great!

When you have returned to full consciousness after the vision of love has been induced, attempt to hold the images in your mind as long as you can. It is important that you hold the thought-forms as long as possible so that you can impress the energy of angelic love upon your Earth plane reality.

The vision images of love and light will open your heart and mind so completely that they will soon condense into the patterns which you are visualizing.

Sometimes after a particularly profound and moving vision of love, you may feel a compulsion to share the essential message of your vision—especially with your love partner. Do so. In such a case, each time you share the vision of love with another, you will receive even more details of the vision and more insight into their specific meaning.

You will clearly know when a vision has been intended only as an individualized instruction strictly for you and should not be described to another.

Twenty-two

The Healing Colors
of the Angels of Love

Since this guided visualization deals with color and with repetitious progressions, it is easy to memorize, so that you can place yourself in a state of deep relaxation. As with the other exercises in this book, you may wish to have a like-minded loved one read the process to you and guide you through the visualization. Or, as before, you may prefer to record a cassette of your own voice ahead of time and thereby serve as your own guide through the experience.

Once again I recommend that you play a recording of the proper music to suggest a mood of lifting yourself away from your mundane environment. Any music that you find inspirational will do— as long as it does not contain any lyrics to distract you from the goal of the exercise.

Sit in a chair, lie on your bed, lean against a wall— whatever position is most comfortable for you. As always when performing these exercises, select a time when you are certain not to be disturbed.

Visualize that at your feet lies a blanket the color of rose. The color of rose stimulates your natural body warmth and induces relaxation and sleep. It can also provide you with a sense of well-being and a marvelous feeling of being loved.

Now you see that the blanket is really a kind of auric cover, a rose-colored auric cover that has been created by the Angels of Love.

Visualize an Angel of Love slowly moving the blanketlike aura of rose up over your body.

Feel the Angel of Love moving the blanket of rose over your feet . . . relaxing them. Over your legs . . . relaxing them. Over your stomach . . . easing all tensions. Over your chest, your arms, your neck . . . relaxing them, relaxing them.

Now see the Angel of Love fashioning a hood of the rose-colored auric energy. Visualize the angel bringing the rose-colored aura over your head. *Feel* the color of rose permeating your psyche and activating your ability to become one with the Angels of Love.

The color green serves as a disinfectant, a cleanser. It also influences the proper building of muscle and tissue.

Visualize an Angel of Love pulling a green, blanketlike aura over your body. Feel it moving over your feet, cleansing them. Feel it moving over your legs, healing them of all pain. Feel it moving over your stomach, ridding it of all discomfort and irritation.

Feel the color of green moving over your chest, your arms, your neck— cleansing them, healing them.

Now see the Angel of Love fashioning a hood of the green-colored auric energy. Visualize the angel bringing the green-colored aura over your head. *Feel* the color of green permeating your psyche and activating your ability to become one with the Angels of Love.

* * *

Gold has been recognized as a great strengthener of the nervous system. Visualizing the color of gold can aid your digestion and help you to become calm.

Visualize now that an Angel of Love is pulling a soft, beautiful golden aura slowly over your body. Feel it moving over your feet, calming your entire body. Feel the color of gold moving over your legs, relaxing them. Feel it moving over your stomach, soothing any nervous condition.

Feel the color of gold moving over your chest, your arms, your neck—strengthening them, calming them.

Now see the Angel of Love fashioning a hood of the gold-colored auric energy. Visualize the angel bringing the gold-colored aura over your head. *Feel* the color of gold permeating your psyche and strengthening your body-brain network so that it will serve as a better conduit for the Angels of Love.

Research has determined that red-orange strengthens and cleanses the lungs. Yogis and other masters have long understood that proper meditation can best be achieved through proper techniques of breathing through clean lungs.

Visualize before you a little red-orange-colored cloud of pure oxygen.

Take a comfortably deep breath and visualize some of that little red-orange cloud moving into your lungs.

Imagine it traveling through your lungs, cleansing them, purifying them, taking away particles of impurities.

Now visualize yourself *exhaling* that red-orange cloud of oxygen from your lungs. See how soiled with impurities it is.

Take another comfortably deep breath. Visualize as you inhale that you are taking a little more of that little red-orange cloud into your lungs.

Imagine it traveling through your lungs, purifying them of the negative effects of exhaust fumes, cigarette smoke, and other pollution.

Exhale the impurities— then breathe again of the purifying, cleansing red-orange cloud.

Research has demonstrated that the color yellow-orange has the ability to aid oxygen in moving into every organ and gland of the human body, purifying them, cleansing them.

Imagine before you now a yellow-orange cloud of pure oxygen.

Take a comfortably deep breath and inhale the cleansing, purifying yellow-orange cloud into your lungs.

Feel the yellow-orange cloud moving through your body. Feel it cleansing and purifying every gland.

If you have *any* area of weakness or disease *anywhere* in your body, *feel* the yellow-orange energy bathing it in cleansing, healing vibrations.

As you exhale all impurities and inhale again the pure yellow-orange cloud of oxygen, visualize the cleansing and healing process throughout your body.

As you exhale and inhale, see your body becoming pure and clean.

Blue is the color of psychic ability, the color that increases visionary potential.

Visualize the Angel of Love moving a blue blanketlike aura over your body. Feel it moving over your feet, relaxing them. Feel the auric cover of blue moving over your legs, soothing them. Feel it moving over your stomach, easing all tensions.

Feel the vibration of blue moving over your

chest, your arms, your neck— soothing them, relaxing them.

Visualize the angel fashioning a hood of the blue-colored auric energy. *Feel* the color of blue permeating your psyche, activating your ability to develop such gifts of the Angels of Love as prophecy, healing, telepathy, and clairvoyance.

Violet is the color of the highest vibration.

Visualize the Angel of Love pulling a violet, blanketlike aura over your body.

Feel it moving over your feet, relaxing them. Feel the color of violet moving over your legs, relaxing them, soothing them. Feel it moving over your stomach, removing all tensions.

Feel the vibration of violet moving over your chest, your arms, your neck— tranquilizing them, relaxing them.

Now visualize the Angel of Love fashioning a hood of the violet-colored auric energy. *Feel* the color of violet permeating your psyche, activating your ability to become one with the Angels of Love.

Feel the color of violet attuning your psyche to the highest heavenly vibration.

Feel the color of violet connecting your psyche to the Source of All-That-Is.

Feel the color of violet permitting you to become one with the Light and the Angels of Love.

*Using the Violet Light
from the Angels of Love
to Transform Any Negativity
That You May Have Sown*

Numerous teachers have said that the violet light that issues from the Source of All-That-Is and the Angels of Love constitutes the highest vibratory level.

There are moments on the Earth plane when, in the course of our day-to-day existence, we may clumsily and thoughtlessly transgress against others. Summoning the violet light from the Angels of Love can assist you in balancing your account. It can help you to *transform* the negativity that you may have sown.

Certain masters have likened the violet light to a cosmic eraser. When you learn to use it often and properly, you may "erase" all elements from your personal vibrations that are not of the Light and of Love.

Other teachers have said that the violet light from the Angels of Love may be used to dissolve disease, to alleviate suffering, and to cure illness.

Disease, suffering, and illness are, after all, manifestations of chaos and discord. Suffusing them with the violet light of love may alter them and raise their vibratory levels to points of transformation.

You may wish to use the violet light of the Angels of Love in a kind of daily ritual of transformation.

Call for the violet light and ask that your angelic guide connect you to the energy of the Angels of Love.

Visualize the violet light moving over you in a wave of warmth.

See it touching every part of your body.

Feel it interacting with each cell.

Say inwardly or aloud to your angelic guide:

"Beloved angel guide, assist me in calling upon the highest of energies and the Source of All-That-Is. Activate the energy of the Angels of Love within me so that I may receive the power and love of the Oneness.

"Provoke the law of harmony for myself who has strayed from the Light and transgressed against another.

"Permit the violet light to move around me and through me. Allow the transforming energy of angelic love to purify and to elevate all impure desires, incorrect concepts, anger, greed, wrongdoings, and improper actions.

"Keep the light of the Angels of Love bright within me.

"Replace all chaotic vibrations around me and *in* me with pure energy, the power of Love, and the harmony of the Divine Plan."

Twenty-three

The Search for
the Divine Soulmate

Some years ago while visiting the Chicago psychic-sensitive Teddy O'Hearn, I asked her if Spirit had given her any teachings concerning the idea of the search for the divine soulmate. Her guidance provided the following message:

"Mark this well, there is a great tapestry being woven as each of us entwines our lives with the other in our journey through the Earthwalk.

"This tapestry is, at one and same time, a record of the past, as well as a means for each thread— each person— to evolve and to reach that perfection in an evolution which will free the individual from Earth's tapestry— and the further necessity of returning to its travail. Woven into this tapestry are ugliness, horror, agony, suffering, and tears, as well as beauty, joy, a measure of fulfillment, and happiness. As in all of nature, nothing is ever lost.

"Only by experiencing the depths of what is inherent in the lowest can we reach the heights of the mystical ecstasy— the union with God and our divinely ordained other half, our soulmate— which transcends beyond imagination anything possible in earthly experience.

"Regardless of the name one bears in any one Earth lifetime, each of us has the eternal 'I' which carries either the male or the female connotation of the androgynous being which we all were in the beginning, before Adam and Eve.

"The separation of the sexes came at that point in time depicted by the Bible's symbolic story of Adam, wherein God made the androgynous Adam two— male and female, plus and minus, negative and positive, Adam and Eve.

"At this time, Earth's beings evolved into self-consciousness. This was not a fall from

Grace, but a further step in human evolution in order that the male and female counterparts of each entity might experience and learn and eventually be reunited when they had evolved through the testing of Earth experience and attained the point at which each had earned the right to a reunion with his divine other half.

"This is the true soulmate, the only 'other' that each of us can look forward to meeting one day. It is with the soulmate that we will share complete fulfillment, a fulfillment beyond anything which we may ever know in any relationship on Earth.

"Our conscious mind may have long since forgotten its soulmate, but the soul memory that we have of our divine 'other half' filters through, though dimly, to our consciousness and leads us to a constant yearning and searching for complete and loving fulfillment which may continue life after life. It is this search which provides us with the means whereby we learn that love is not possession, that love is not self-serving, that love is not tyrannical or cruel, that love is not sex alone in any of its ramifications.

"We learn by trial and error through many loves and many lives— often encountering the same soulmates over and over again. All of these mates are soulmates by reason of the mutual learning process which takes place, but they must not be confused with the 'divine' soulmate—both halves of which are seldom encountered in the physical Earth plane. Each of these earthly soulmate relationships must be transmitted, from disharmony into harmony, into true universal love.

"We must learn real love through giving and receiving, of dealing with imitations and misconceptions of the real thing in order to achieve a complete education in love which will make us fit for the reunion with the divine soulmate.

"Thus our searching and learning process may take us through many lifetimes in which we encounter many of the same 'loves' over and over again, sometimes as parents, as sisters, as brothers, as children, as friends, as enemies, as business associates, as teachers, as students, as well as lovers and husbands and wives.

"Our relationship with any one other individual is a learning experience and a perfection of the many facets of love. When we have learned and earned the right, we will begin to realize that love is indeed universal, rather than personal—that love, tempered by wisdom, is the tool we have to carry with us in our release from our earthly lives.

"When we progress to the next step on the

ladder and achieve the reunion and the fulfillment of self in the personal love of our
divine soulmate, the two of us— as One— will
go on into the fulfillment of ourselves in the
work of God."

Author's Note

Many of the people who contributed their own experiences with the Angels of Love also happen to be men and women who offer their own research, counsel, artistic expression or inspiration to those who seek more information about angelic interaction with Earth's mortal citizens.

For further details, readers may contact these individuals directly at the addresses below:

Lori Jean and Charles Flory, Post Office Box 1328, Conifer, Colorado 80433.

Vera and Joshua Shapiro, V&J Enterprises (The Peruvian Connection) 9737 Fox Glen Dr. #1K, Niles, Illinois 60714.

Jon Marc and Anastasia Hammer, Heartlight, Post Office Box 22877, Santa Fe, New Mexico 87502-2877.

Lois and Clay East, Angelic Images, Post Office Box 280843, Lakewood, Colorado 80228.

Lorraine Darr, 685 Dorchester Drive, Dorchester, Iowa 52140-7603.

David and Barbara Jungclaus, Lost World Publishing, 2899 Agoura Road, Suite 381, Westlake Village, California 91361.

Judith Richardson Haimes, Pentacle Publications, 10710 Seminole Blvd. Suite #3, Seminole, Florida 34648.

John Harricharan, 1401 Johnson Ferry Road, Suite 328-M7, Marrietta, Georgia 30062.

Moi-RA and RA-Ja Dove, Rose Petals Star Ranch Community of Light, 268 Rome Road, Lancing, Tennessee 37770.

Those readers who wish to share their own angelic or mystical experiences may obtain a copy of the *Steiger Questionnaire of Mystical, Paranormal, and UFO Experiences* by sending a stamped, self-addressed, business envelope to Sherry and Brad Steiger, Timewalker Productions, Post Office Box 434, Forest City, Iowa 50436.